ART DIRECTORS' INDEX
TO ILLUSTRATORS
18

RotoVision

CREDITS · COPYRIGHT

COVER IMAGE

HAMZA ARCAN

The Studio

1 Salisbury Road

HOVE

BN3 3AB

UK

Tel: +44 (0) 1273 205030

Fax: +44 (0) 1273 720373

COVER DESIGN

CLIVE SPRING

PUBLISHER

ROTOVISION SA

7 Rue du Bugnon

CH 1299 Crans

Switzerland

Tel: +41 22 776 0511

Fax: +41 22 776 0889

SALES OFFICE:

Sheridan House

112-116A Western Road

Hove

East Sussex

BN3 1DD

United Kingdom

Tel: +44 (0) 1273 727268

Fax: +44 (0) 1273 727269

COPYRIGHT

© 1998 ROTOVISION SA

ISBN 2-88046-320-3

Printed in Hong Kong

CONTENTS

PORTFOLIO OF PAGE SALES AGENTS

ARGENTINA
Aquiles Ferrario
Documenta SRL
Córdoba 612 entrepiso
1054
Buenos Aires
Argentina
Tel: +54 1 332 9581
Fax: +54 1 326 9595

BELGIUM
Koen de Witte
Foto Art
Nieuwe Gentweg 148
B 8000 Brugge
Belgium
Tel: +32 50 33 05 32
Fax: + 32 50 34 61 53

BRAZIL
Hirokazu Taguchi,
Casa Ono Comércio e Importção Ltda
Rua Fernao Dias 492
Pinheiros
CEP 05427
Sau Paulo SP Brazil
Tel: +55 11 813 6522
Fax: +55 11 212 6488

FRANCE
Didier Poupard
Didier Poupard & Associés
19 rue de Bassano
F-75116
Paris
France
Tel: +33 1 47 20 11 13 / 20 22
Fax: +33 1 47 20 55 44

GERMANY
Gudrun Tempelmann-Boehr
Am Rosenbaum 7
D-40699
Erkrath
Germany
Tel: +49 211 25 32 46
Fax: +49 211 25 46 32

GERMANY
Margret Ostrowski-Wenzel
Am Weiher 14
D-20255
Hamburg
Germany
Tel: +49 40 40 56 12
Fax: +49 40 40 56 12

GERMANY
Jörg Seidl & Harald Kling
GKK Frankfurt
Poseidon Haus
Theodor-Heuss-Allee 2
D-60486
Frankfurt A.M.
Germany
Tel: +49 69 75 44 75
Fax: +49 69 75 44 77

ITALY
Zandra Mantilla
Via Monte Amiata 3
I-20149 Milano
Italy
Tel: +39 2 498 4926 / 480 12684
Fax: +39 2 498 4926

MEXICO
María Elena Trujillo
InterBooks
Juan Escutia #42 - Locales E
F y G Col. Condesa
06140
Mexico
DF Mexico
Tel: +52 5 553 1845
Fax: +52 5 553 1244

MEXICO
Visualibros
Xototi No. 29 B-201
Col. Tlaxpana
11370
Mexico DF
Mexico
Tel: +52 5 566 2111
Fax: +52 5 535 7986
Email: visual@ibm.net

NETHERLANDS
Koen de Witte
Foto Art
Nieuwe Gentweg 148
B 8000 Brugge
Belgium
Tel: +32 50 33 05 32
Fax: + 32 50 34 61 53

SCANDINAVIA
Barbro Ehn
BOE Media AB
Sibyllegatan 38
114 43 Stockholm
Sweden
Tel: +46 8 661 0069
Fax: +46 8 661 0073

SINGAPORE
John Cheong
Associate Media Pte Ltd
35 Tannery Road
#06-01 Tannery Block
Ruby Ind Complex
347740 Singapore
Tel: +65 842 5136
Fax: +65 742 6933
Email: asmedia@pacific.net.sg

SLOVENIA
Andrej Jerovsek
Kodia Photo & Graphis d.o.c.
Zelenapot 23
1000 Ljubljana
Slovenia
Tel: +386 61 331 705
Fax: +386 61 331 705

SOUTH AFRICA
Trudy Dickens
Association of Marketers
P.O. Box 98853
Sloane Park
2152 Johannesburg
South Africa
Tel: +27 11 462 2380 / 706 1633
Fax: +27 11 706 4151

SPAIN
Sylvie Estrada
Index Book SL
Consell de Cent 160 - Local 3
E-08015
Barcelona
Spain
Tel: +3493 454 5547
Fax: +3493 454 8438
Email: ib@indexbook.com

SWITZERLAND
Katja Cavazzi
T-Case AG
Zollikerstrasse 19
Postfach CH-8032
Zürich
Switzerland
Tel: +41 1 383 4680
Fax: +41 1 383 4680

UK
Joyce Quinnell
RotoVision
Sheridan House
112/116a Western Road
Hove BN3 1DD
East Sussex
UK
Tel: +44 (0)1273 716021
Fax: +44 (0)1273 727269
Email: creative@rotovision.com

REGIONAL OFFICES:

ASIA
Alice Goh
ProVision Pte Ltd
34 Wilkie Road
228054 Singapore
Tel: +65 334 7720
Fax: +65 334 7721
Email: prov@pacific.net.sg

SOUTH AMERICA
Alejandro Christe
Delegación América Latina
Alsina 120
5147 Argüello
Córdoba Argentina
Tel: +54 543 20925
Fax: +54 543 20925
Email: christe@arnet.com.ar

A U S T R A L I A

I L L U S T R A T I O N

UPHAM-HILL Studios

PERTH, WESTERN AUSTRALIA
tel. & fax. (61 8) 9276 7775

• • • • • • • • • • • • • •

CRAIG UPHAM-HILL
B. Arch Hons.

Professional Architectural Illustrating and Visualising

FRANCE

ILLUSTRATION

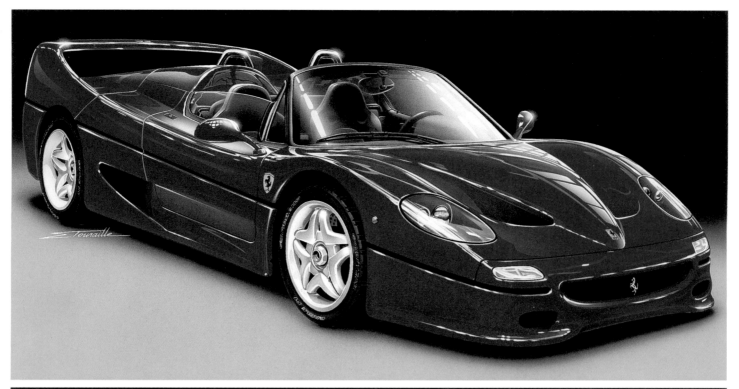

ERIC TOURAILLE CREATIONS

■ ■ ■ ■ ■ ■ ■ ■ ■ ■ ■ ■ ■ ■ ■

«Les Martines Nord»
69290 POLLIONNAY
FRANCE

Société créée en 1986   **TÉL: 33 (0)4 78 48 13 34**   *Spécialisé en aérographie hyperréaliste*
Activités: **FAX 33 (0)4 78 48 14 08**   *Editions d'art : lithographies,*
Illustration, Graphisme   *cartes postales, posters,*
Edition, Packaging...   *calendriers, etc...*

GERMANY

ILLUSTRATION

ERIKA MOOS-DREVENSTEDT
ILLUSTRATION+DESIGN

Paul-Gerhardt-Str.23 / D-47877 Willich
Telefon: +49-(0)2156-3806 / Fax: +49-(0)2156-1380
Mobil: +49 (0)172-2105700

Freelance since 1969. Figurative, cartoon, plants, animals, computer   Selbständig seit 1969. Figürliches, Cartoon, Pflanzen, Tiere, Computer

agent: gudrun Tempelmann-boehr tel.: 0211

T 49[0]211 55 71 21 6

F A X 49[0]211 55 71 21 8

4 05 45 DÜSSELDORF KAISER WILHELM RING 19

http://www.uertz.mcs.de

e—mail: p_uertz@mail.mcs.de

PETER Uertz

J A P A N

I L L U S T R A T I O N

Strong Wind

I like the palm tree.

*It stands there gracefully, totally entrusting
just its leaves to the strong wind.*

*It probably knows the strong wind will drop its fruit
and continue to increase its companions.*

Hope and Despair

*When you truly desire them, wings seem to sprout
before you know it.
But it's better not to despair when you realise you can't have wings.*

*That is because in place of wings,
you'll most likely acquire a warmth like down towards others.*

Back Stage

Devote yourself to something you like to do.

*The strong beam of the spotlight
and the applause of the masses could be waiting for you.*

*But when, all alone backstage,
you wipe away the perspiration on your forehead,
I will be waiting for you.*

MASAHIKO IKEDA
● ● ● ● ● ● ● ● ● ●

*1-6-34#302
Minami-azabu Minato-ku
Tokyo 106-0047
Japan
Tel: +81 3 5445 4339
Fax: +81 3 5445 4340*

MARIKO ABE

- - - - - - - - - - - - -

Palace Yoyogiuehara 402
3-1-8 Nishihara
Shibuya-ku
Tokyo 151-0066
Japan
Tel: +81 3 3465 4048
Fax: +81 3 3262 9463

MARIKO ABE

Palace Yoyogiuehara 402
3-1-8 Nishihara
Shibuya-ku
Tokyo 151-0066
Japan
Tel: +81 3 3465 4048
Fax: +81 3 3262 9463

MASATO ARAI

• • • • • • • • • • •

Pictogram Illustration
8-9-6 Shakujii-cho
Nerima-ku
Tokyo 177-0041
Japan
Tel: (03) 3996 0676
Fax: (03) 3996 9496

MASATO ARAI

• • • • • • • • • • • •

Pictogram Illustration
8-9-6 Shakujii-cho
Nerima-ku
Tokyo 177-0041
Japan
Tel: (03) 3996 0676
Fax: (03) 3996 9496

NALIHICO JOYA

- - - - - - - - - - - -

68 Asahigaoka Kanagawa-ku
Yokohama-shi
Kanagawa 221-0814
Japan
Tel: +81 45 481 4557
Fax: +81 45 481 4557

NALIHICO JOYA

◆◆◆◆◆◆◆◆◆◆◆◆

68 Asahigaoka Kanagawa-ku
Yokohama-shi
Kanagawa 221-0814
Japan
Tel: +81 45 481 4557
Fax: +81 45 481 4557

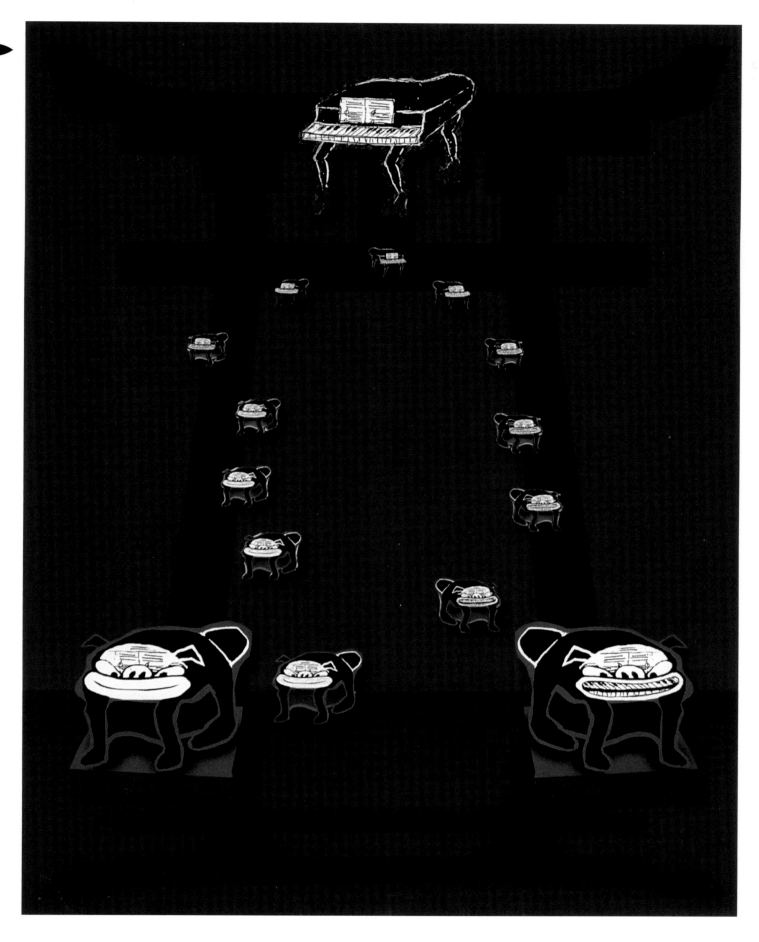

YOSHIMI KASANO

•••••••••••••

5-47-1 #101
Yoyogi Shibuya-ku
Tokyo 151
Japan
Tel: 03 5454 2957
Fax: 03 5454 2957

MASAKO MISAKI
● ● ● ● ● ● ● ● ● ● ● ●

2-4-27 Kasumi-chou
Yamagata City
Yamagata-ken 990-0039
Japan
Tel: (0236) 41-0552
Fax: (0236) 41-0552

2-38-2 Todoroki
Setagaya-ku
Tokyo 158-0082
Japan
Tel: (03) 3702 3877
Fax: (03) 3702 3877

Pssst ! Bleibt Still ! Jetzt passt mal auf !
Das neue Leben ist endlich da.
Liebevoll wollen wir nun fur es sorgen.
-Das ist eine Geschichte auf einem winzig kleinen
Planeten, der in der Ecke des grenzenlosen
Universums schimmernd sein Dasein hat.
しーっ　おしゃべりしないで　そっとこっちをむいて。
ほらわ！あたらしい　いのちがうまれたよ。
たいせつにそだててゆこうよ。
ひろいうちゅうのかたすみの
ぴっかりひかるちいさなほしの
できごとです。

JYOKO KUBO
- - - - - - - - - -

1-37-73 Shiohama
Higashi-ku Fukuoka-shi
Fukuoka 811-0203
Japan
Tel: 092 608 2900
Fax: 092 608 2900

JYOKO KUBO

• • • • • • • • • • •

1-37-73 Shiohama
Higashi-ku Fukuoka-shi
Fukuoka 811-0203
Japan
Tel: 092 608 2900
Fax: 092 608 2900

Using Adobe Dimensions™ & Adobe Illustrator™

Using Adobe Illustrator™

TOSHINAO KUMAGAI

3-16-32-1 . E
Kouenji-minami Suginami-ku
Tokyo 166-0003
Japan
Tel: 03 3313 8358
Fax: 03 3313 9936

Using Adobe Illustrator™

Using Shade Professional™ & Adobe Photoshop™

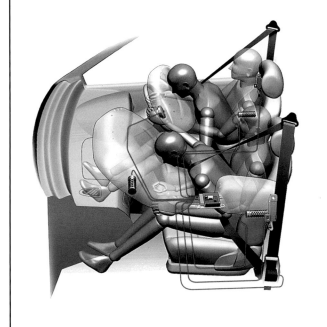

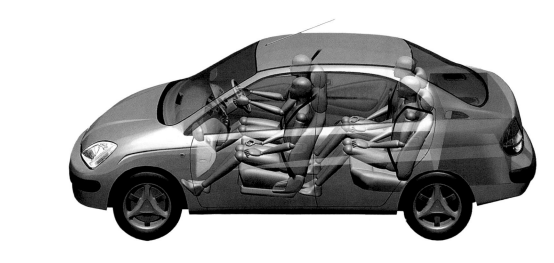

TOSHINAO KUMAGAI

3-16-32-1 . E
Kouenji-minami Suginami-ku
Tokyo 166-0003
Japan
Tel: 03 3313 8358
Fax: 03 3313 9936

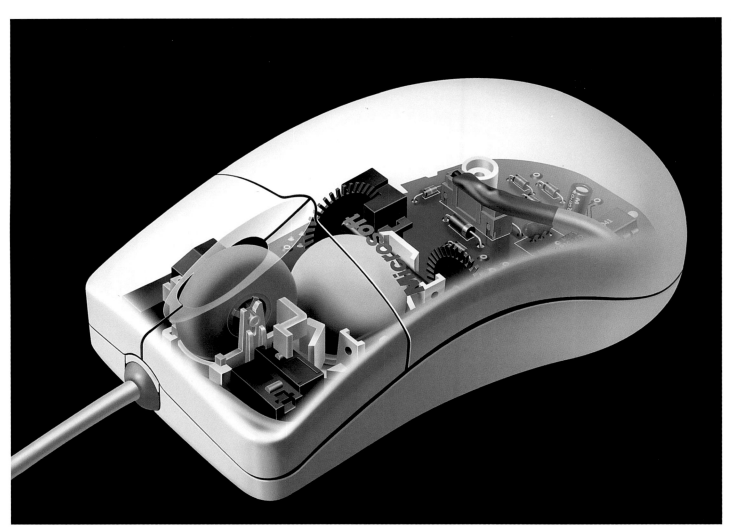

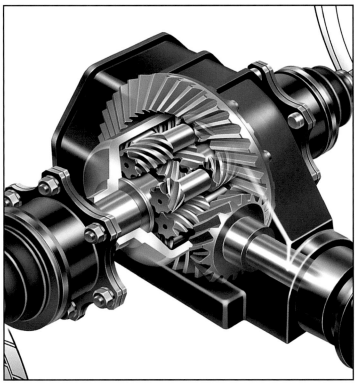

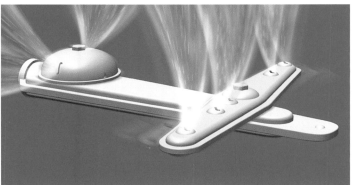

HIDE NAKAJIMA
• • • • • • • • • • • • •

410-8 Kameino
Fujisawa-shi
Kanagawa 252-0813
Japan
Tel: 0466 82 9638
Fax: 0466 82 4984

SHUJI TERADA

- - - - - - - - -

2-144-4 Senzo
Itami-shi
Hyogo 664-0898
Japan
Tel: +81 727 79 2297
Fax: +81 727 79 2297

EIJI TAMURA

• • • • • • • • • • • •

Shakujii Hightraise 1004
1-11-5 Takanodai
Nerima-ku Tokyo 177-0033
Japan
Tel: +81 3 3996 4312
Fax: +81 3 3996 4312

EIJI TAMURA
• • • • • • • • • • • • •

Shakujii Hightraise 1004
1-11-5 Takanodai
Nerima-ku Tokyo 177-0033
Japan
Tel: +81 3 3996 4312
Fax: +81 3 3996 4312

HIROSHI YOSHII
• • • • • • • • • • •

1-2-13-304 Tamagawadai
Setagaya-ku
Tokyo 158-0096
Japan
Tel: +81 3 5491 5337
Fax: +81 3 5491 5337
hiroshi@yoshii.com
http://www.yoshii.com/

HIROSHI YOSHII

1-2-13-304 Tamagawadai
Setagaya-ku
Tokyo 158-0096
Japan
Tel: +81 3 5491 5337
Fax: +81 3 5491 5337
hiroshi@yoshii.com
http://www.yoshii.com/

TETSUO USHIJIMA
• • • • • • • • • •

3-10-2-1202 Toyosaki
Kita-ku
Osaka 531-0072
Japan
Tel: 06 373 6127
Fax: 06 373 6127

B R A Z I L

I L L U S T R A T I O N

I L U S T R A C I Ó N

! – *Charge. FHC. Inédito, 1/12/1997*

Charge. FHC. Unpublished Works

Caricature. FHC. Inédit

2 – *Piada para revista de Passatempos.*

Abril de 1997

Joke bound for a Pastime Magazine.

April of 1997

Saillie pour la révue (Passatempos).

Avril 1997

André Barroso

- - - - - - - - - - - - -

r. Dionísio Erthal 13 sobrado – Santa Rosa
Niterói / Rio de Janeiro /Brasil
CEP: 24240–020
TEL: (021) 7171817

3 – *Ilustração para o caderno de Empregos. O Dia,*

8/06/1997

Ilustration bound for job section of O Dia diary

Illustration pour le journal O Dia

4 – *Ilustração para o livro infantil Gagaguinho.*

Ed. Armazém de idéias. Julho de 1995

Ilustration bound for Gagaguinho, an intile

book. Armazém de Idéias publishing. 1995 july

Illustration pour livre enfantin Gagaguinho,

les éditions Armazém de Idéias. Juillet, 1995

ESTÚDIO T ARTE & ANIMAÇÃO PUBLICITÁRIA LTDA

- - - - - - - - - - -

*Rua Treze de Maio
1016 Bela Vista
São Paulo SP 01327-020
Brazil
Tel: +55 11 288 7388
Fax: +55 11 288 7596
www.estudiot.com.br*

ESTÚDIO T
ARTE & ANIMAÇÃO

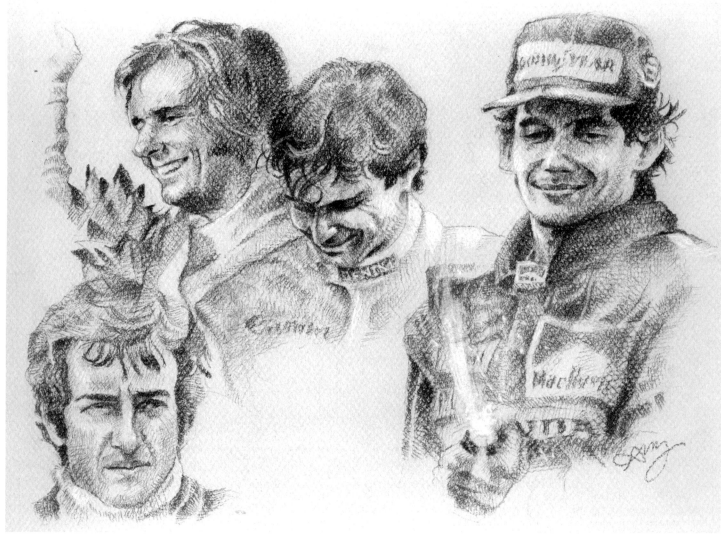

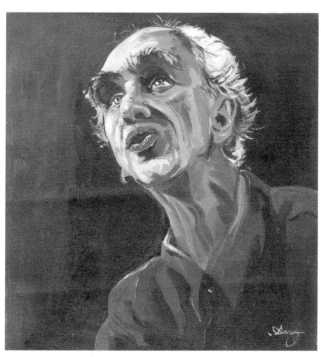

ARY MORAES
– • – • – • – • – • – • –
(021) 528 - 0528
CODE: 106 - 8248
Rio de Janeiro - Brasil
(021) 261 -2845

Infografia	Planejamento Visual	Ilustração
Infografia	Diseño	Dibujo
Informational Graphics	Graphic Design	Illustration

COSTA RICA

ILLUSTRATION

ILUSTRACIÓN

MARIO PERAZA M.
• • • • • • • • • •

PERAZA STUDIO
San José Costa Rica
Tel: (506) 283-2902/ (506) 380-5602/ Fax: (506) 224-3298

Http//www.rhed.co.cr/peraza
e-mail: peraza@rhed.co.cr

Ilustración digital, manual, caricatura, comics
Diseño Publicitario y Asesoría en Imagen Corporativa.

JOHN TIMMS

Animastudio S.A.
Apdo: 10728-1000
San José Costa Rica
Tel/Fax: +506 227 2216
Email: jtimms@interwebcr.com

THE NETHERLANDS

ILLUSTRATION

INGRID BAARS
• • • • • • • • • •

Noordmolenwerf 89
NL 3011 DC
Rotterdam
Tel: +31 10 213 4095
Fax: +31 10 411 9501

Use: Annual Report
Client: Cap Gemini

Represented by Art box, Amsterdam

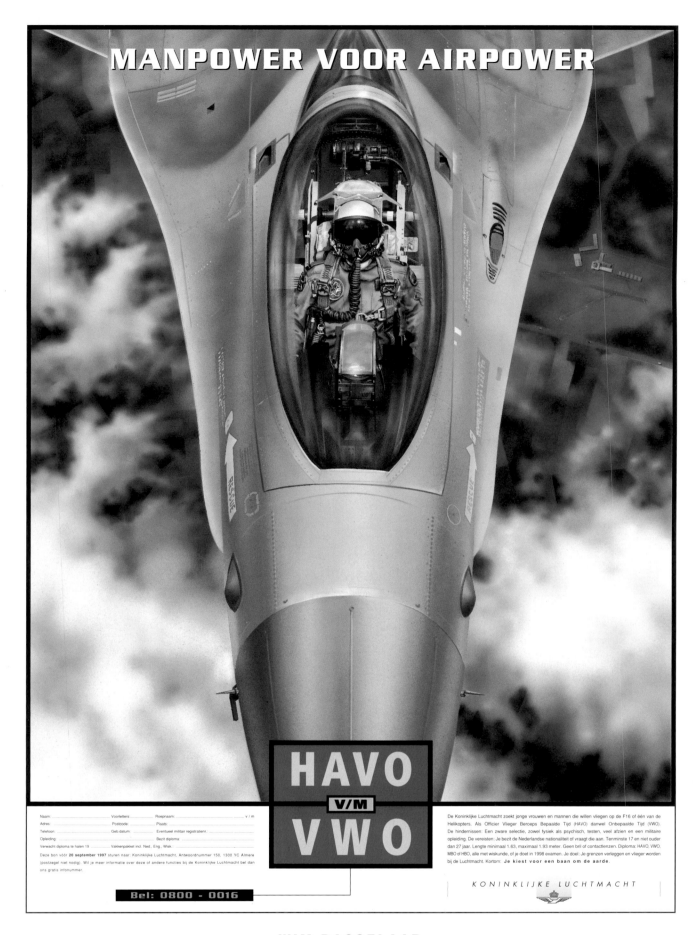

MANPOWER VOOR AIRPOWER

HAVO
V/M
VWO

Bel: 0800 - 0016

De Koninklijke Luchtmacht zoekt jonge vrouwen en mannen die willen vliegen op de F16 of één van de Helikopters. Als Officier Vlieger Beroeps Bepaalde Tijd (HAVO) danwel Onbepaalde Tijd (VWO). De hindernissen: Een zware selectie, zowel fysiek als psychisch, testen, veel afzien en een militaire opleiding. De vereisten: Je bezit de Nederlandse nationaliteit of vraagt die aan. Tenminste 17 en niet ouder dan 27 jaar. Lengte minimaal 1.63, maximaal 1.93 meter. Geen bril of contactlenzen. Diploma: HAVO, VWO, MBO of HBO, alle met wiskunde, of je doet in 1998 examen. Je doel: Je grenzen verleggen en vlieger worden bij de Luchtmacht. Kortom: **Je kiest voor een baan om de aarde.**

KONINKLIJKE LUCHTMACHT

WIM DASSELAAR

Base-Line C.V.
Rijksstraatweg 124
9752 BK Haren
Netherlands
Tel / Fax: +31 (0) 50 57 35 351
e-mail:wimd@noord.bart.nl

Client: Dutch Royal Airforce

Technique: Airbrush

HESTER DAPPER
● ● ● ● ● ● ● ● ● ● ● ●

Studio van Dapperen
Brouwers Gracht 86
1013 GZ Amsterdam
Netherlands
Tel / Fax: +31 (20) 625 2846
Mobile: 0651 658968

Freelance illustrator and painter

  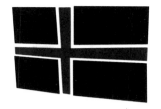 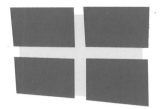

DENMARK FINLAND NORWAY SWEDEN

ILLUSTRATION

AABECH, FLEMMING
Jægersborg Alle 16, 2920 Charlottenlund, 39 64 41 47, Fax: 39 64 51 57

LEIF ABJORNSSEN

Kaptensg. 11 n.b
114 57 Stockholm
Sweden
Tel: +46 8 6622525
Fax: +46 8 6603446

ULLA ALMQUIST

• • • • • • • • • • • •

Almquist AB
Box 35, 430 94 Bohus-Björkö, Sweden
Tel: +46 31 929072   Fax: +46 31 929073
E-mail: reklam@almquistab.se

1. *Newsletter. Client: Kulturdepartementet*
2. *Streamer. Client: Aldéns*
3. *Logo. Client: AlfaKonsult*

4. *Web Design. Client: Mölndals kommun*
5. *Published. Client: Self-promotion*
6. *Comics. Client: Göteborgs Stad*

7. *Illustration for courses and seminars. Client: SIK*
8. *Unpublished. Client: Self-promotion*

JOHANNE EMILIE ANDERSEN
● ● ● ● ● ● ● ● ● ●

Basta,
Thv. Meyers Gate 56
0552 Oslo
Norway
Tel: +47 22 351111
Fax: +47 22 870913

Illustrasjoner til Regnbuekalenderen 95. Utgitt av Antirasistisk Senter. Tusj, papirklipp.

1

2

MARITA ANDERSEN

● ● ● ● ● ● ● ● ● ● ● ●

Vesle-Vollaug
2032 Maura
Norway
Tel: +47 63 993069
Fax: +47 63 993015

1-2 Upublisert/skolebok. Akryl.

TERESE J. ANDERSEN

Satiretegning
Layouts
Storyboards

ART DIRECTOR / ILLUSTRATOR
Holger Danskes Vej 83 Kld. • DK. 2000 Frederiksberg • Tlf./fax: +45 38 88 38 60

Olieill.
Airbrushill.
Akvarelill.

1

2

TROND ANDERSSON

"Teiknestugu"
3570 Ål.
Norway
Tel: +47 32 081111
Tel: +47 32 081308
Fax: +47 32 1565

1. Illustrasjon til eske for "Trollungen". Brusletto. Fargeblyant.   2. Illustrasjon til julekort. Hallingdølen. Fargeblyant.

2

RANDI ANDREASSEN
• • • • • • • • • • • •

Majorstuveien 26
0367 Oslo
Norway
Tel: +47 22 563293

Four Seasons, Vivaldi, Blandningsteknikk på egg.

Tarjei
VESAAS
Kimen

Tarjei
VESAAS
Fuglane

Tarjei
VESAAS
Is-slottet

Tarjei
VESAAS
Båten om kvelden

INGER SANDVED ANFINSEN
• • • • • • • • • •

Semafor
Pilestredet 27, N-0164 Oslo, Norway
Tel: +47 22 112936 Fax: +47 22 112889 E-mail: isas@telepost.no

Semafor is a group of five illustrators and designers. We cover visual communication and illustration in fields such as magazine design, book covers and book design, editorial illustration and management, packaging, exhibition design and advertising.

MARIT JØRGENSEN
• • • • • • • • • • •

Semafor
Pilestredet 27, N-0164 Oslo, Norway
Tel: +47 22 203208 Fax: +47 22 112889

Semafor is a group of five illustrators and designers. We cover visual communication and illustration in fields such as magazine design, book covers and book design, editorial illustration and management, packaging, exhibition design and advertising.

Illustration for Amnesty International, Norwegian Section, Christmas card 1997.

Universal Declaration of Human Rights. Article 3:
Everyone has the right to life, liberty and security of person.

SVEIN STØRKSEN
● ● ● ● ● ● ● ● ● ● ● ●

Semafor
Pilestredet 27, N-0164 Oslo, Norway
Tel: +47 22 115668 Fax: +47 22 112889

JOSEF LEUPI

Semafor
Pilestredet 27, N-0164 Oslo, Norway
Tel: +47 22 111093 Fax: +47 22 112889

Semafor is a group of five illustrators and designers. We cover visual communication and illustration in fields such as magazine design, book covers and book design, editorial illustration and management, packaging, exhibition design and advertising.

Illustration & design: Josef Leupi

BØKENES VERDEN

Terry tok Martinez i hånden og grep armen hans. Applausen steg. Celebritetene på podiet reiste seg og klappet voldsomt. De to blendende unge mennene la armene om hverandre og forvandlet håndtrykket til en varm omfavnelse. Mengden nedenfor podiet stod på tå. Og brølet fra folkehopen var så høyrøstet at skuddene ville gått ubemerket hen, som kinaputter i en annen gate, hvis det ikke hadde vært for at kulene lot til å eksplodere idet de traff...

▶▶▶

▶▶▶

Da gikk det opp for ham at det var han selv som var såret, at han måtte være tapper og rakrygget trass i smertene. Han grep hånden hennes og prøvde å reise seg. Men skuddsåret i siden trakk ham ned som et digert lodd, og ban-

kingen i pannen blindet ham og gjorde ham ydmyk. «Ligg rolig, senator!» kommanderte en morsk stemme ved siden av ham. Men han aktet så visst ikke å ligge rolig. Han kjempet seg opp på albuen...

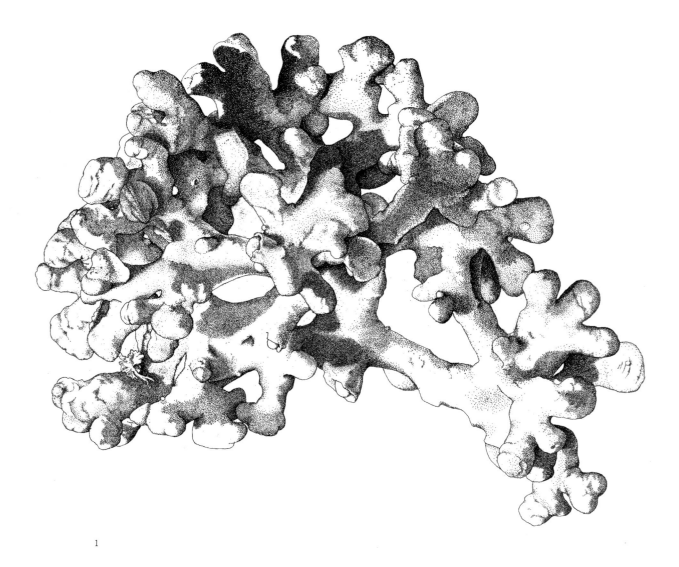

1

KIRSTEN MAGNI DØVRE BANG

Bakkeveien 9D
6100 Volda
Norway
Tel: +47 70 077484
Fax: +47 70 077484

Illustrasjon av kalkalge (Lithothamnion sp.), sterkt forstørret. Tegnet for Institutt for marinbiologi, Universitetet i Bergen. Tusj.

Uno Blaesild • Snabel Design
Vadensjövägen 96   261 91 Landskrona Sweden
Tel: 0418/432117   E-mail: snabel-d@algonet.se

Bang & Olufsen

Dansk Reklame Film
Danish Screen Advertising

TV-A
Danish Broadcasting Corporation

The Danish Chamber of Commerce

DLG
Danish Co-operative Farm Supply

Mac World Magazine

VIVI BARSTED

· · · · · · · · · · ·

Box 543, Horsensgade 19, 8000 Aarhus C, Denmark Tel: +45 86 130386 Fax:+ 45 86 130986 Mobile: +45 20 27 72 20
Email: vivi@inet.uni-c.dk Homepage: http://inet.uni-c.dk/~vivi

Børneplakaten 1997-98

Børns Vilkår
- for børn i Danmark

TELE DANMARK
Støtter Børns Vilkår

Børneplakaten
1997-98 er tegnet af
Vivi Barstød

Flensborg Grafisk A/S

Children's Welfare in Denmark

1

ALF-KAARE BERG
● ● ● ● ● ● ● ● ● ● ● ●

Løkkegaten 1
2200 Kongsvinger
Norway
Tel: +47 62 813286
Fax: +47 62 813286

1. Illustrasjon til krimnovelle i Aftenposten. Mixed media.

2. Presentasjonsillustrasjon for Lars Saabye Christensen bok "Jubel" i Bokspeilet, DnB-klubbene. Mixed media.

BOGDAN BOCIANOWSKI

Atriumveien 11 E
1400 Ski
Norway
Tel: +47 64 872288
Fax: +47 64 872788

Illustrasjon til en krimnovelle "Mannen i parken" av Odd W. Sureén. Gouache, akryl.

GUNNAR BØEN

• • • • • • • • • • • • •

2. Strøm Terrasse 19
3046 Drammen
Norway
Tel: +47 32 895565
Fax: +47 32 895565

Illustrasjon for Bergans. Data (Photoshop)

TROND BREDESEN

Illustratørene
Pilestredet 27
0164 Oslo
Norway
Tel: +47 22 111800
Fax: +47 22 111814

KIM BROSTRÖM
• • • • • • • • • • • • •

Øster Farimagsgade 32, 5
2100 København Ø
Denmark
Tel/Fax: +45 35 384474

Illustration & Graphic Design

Tilde Louise Carlsen, Langegyde 64, 5762 V. Skerninge, Denmark, e-mail Tilde@post4.tele.dk
To see further illustrations look at the internetadress: Illustratorguiden.dk

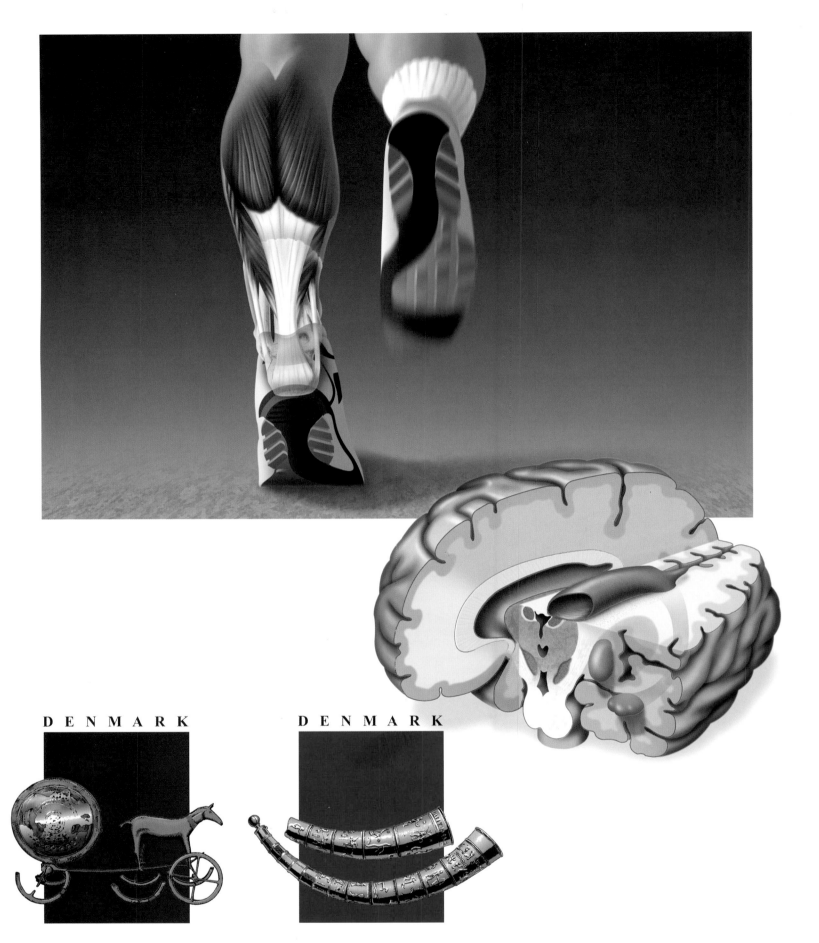

DENMARK DENMARK

HENNING DALHOFF · TORVESTRÆDET 6 · DK-3450 ALLERØD
Tel. +45 48 14 02 03 · Fax +45 48 14 04 46
e-mail: henning@dalhoff.dk · Homepage: www.dalhoff.dk

Jesper
Deleuran

Bøger, blade,
pjecer og andre
tryksager.

Tusch, akvarel o.a.

Stengade 22
2200 København N
Telefon 35 37 38 09
Fax 35 37 38 09

STELLA EAST

Doktorgården
5730 Ulvik
Norway
Tel: +47 56 526633
Fax: +47 56 526633

Book cover for religious and ethical education

JERKER ERIKSSON

• • • • • • • • • •

Illustratör Jerker Eriksson AB
Fersens väg 9
S21142 Malmö
Sweden
Tel: +46 40 300450
Fax: +46 40 301006

On Saturday Night

On Saturday night,
I lost my dog,
and where do you think
I found it?
Up in the moon,
playing a tune,
and all the stars around it.

MARIANNE ERLANDSSON
●●●●●●●●●●●●

Fregattgatan 11
426 74 Västra Frölunda, Sweden
Tel: +46 31 297726
Fax: +46 31 297726
E-mail: marianne.erlandsson@illustration.pp.se

Clients: Publishers (preferably
schoolbooks), advertising
companies and others

Illustrations from various
schoolbooks and adverts.
Techniques: Watercolour, Indian
Ink Pen

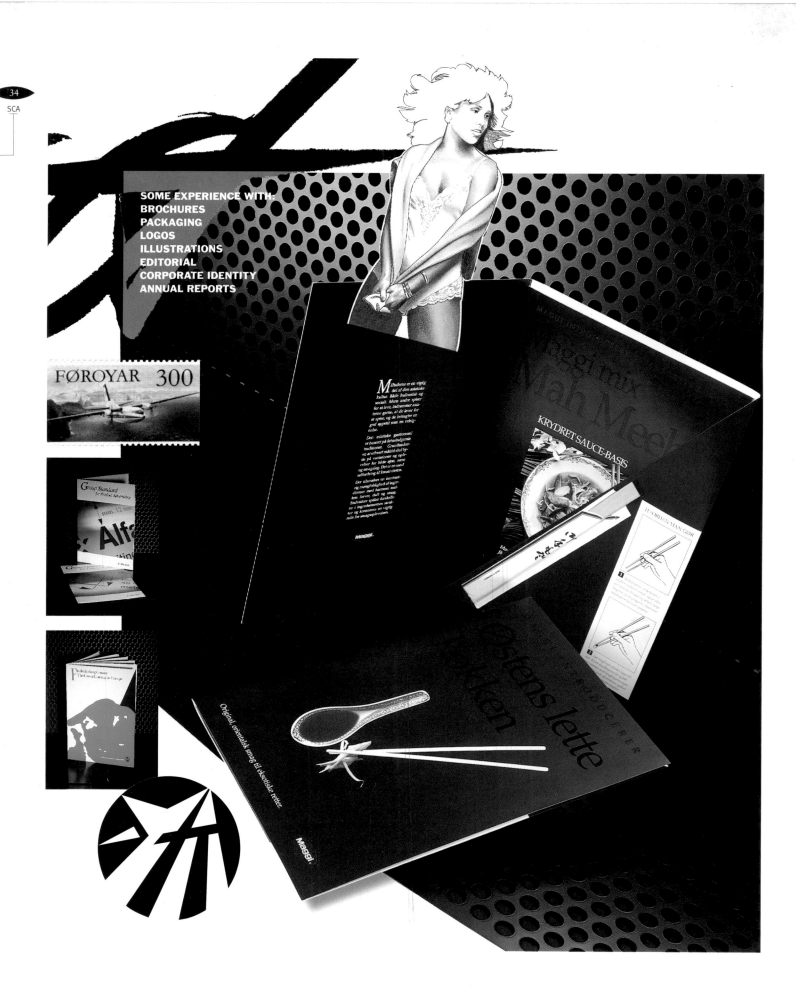

SOME EXPERIENCE WITH:
BROCHURES
PACKAGING
LOGOS
ILLUSTRATIONS
EDITORIAL
CORPORATE IDENTITY
ANNUAL REPORTS

DAN FREDERIKSEN

····················

Gothersgade 93 C
DK-1123 København K. Denmark
Phone/Fax: +45 33 32 45 04

MIA GJERDRUM
••••••••••••

Frederik Stangs Gate 14, 0272 Olso, Norway. Tel: +47 22 562812

"Fred" Elevarrbeid fra Academy of Art Collage, San Francisco. Blyant, penn og Illustrator 6.0

ROLF GRAFF
••••••••••••

Industrigaten 38 B
0357 Oslo
Norway
Tel: +47 22 609533

1. Kampanje NHO (1/6). Mix.   2. Krimillustrasjon Alle Menn. Mix.   3. Telenor (datterbedrifter). Mix.

ANNE KRISTIN HAGESÆTHER
• • • • • • • • • • • •

Tostrups Terrasse 7
0271 Oslo
Norway
Tel: +47 22 55 53 26
Fax: +47 22 55 53 26

ANNETTE HALVORSEN

• • • • • • • • • • • •

Thereses Gate 40
0168 Oslo
Norway
Tel: +47 22 69 76 61

MÅLFRID BERG HANSEN
● ● ● ● ● ● ● ● ● ● ●

Buen 13
1528 Moss
Norway
Tel: +47 69 267245

Upublisert. Collage

STEFAN HANSSON

• • • • • • • • • • • •

Siriusgatan 47
195 55 Märsta
Sweden
Tel: 0859112103
Fax: 0859112103
Mobile: 0708 249436

Several exhibitions in Scandinavia and USA. Books, advertising, background paintings, galleries.
Clients include WWF, SCA, NCC, Philips, Swedish Museum of Natural History, SEMIC. Techniques: watercolour, mixed media, oil and lithographs.

ANE-Bøgerne,
bind 1 - 12

Lille Louise

Novelleillustration
"Min usynlige jul"

Susanna
Hartmann

Håndtegnet
Illustration

Speciale:
Alle slags
børnebøger i
akvarel og sort/hvid.

Toftekærsvej 28 C
2820 Gentofte
Telefon 39 65 89 90
Fax 39 65 89 90

Logodesign

Posters

Illustrations

Webdesign

Covers

Tjek ➡ | http://inet.uni2.dk/home/hedegaard/ |

Hedegaard Grafisk Design

Jørgen Hedegaard MDD
Willemoesgade 9
DK-2100 København Ø
tlf. 31 42 42 90
fax. 31 42 72 82

HILDE HODNEFJELD

●●●●●●●●●●●●

Basta
Thv. Meyers Gate 56
0552 Oslo
Norway
Tel: +47 22 718121
Fax: +47 22 870913
Privat: +47 22 951922

Forside, Den Norsk tannlegeforenings Tidende. Etsning, fargeblyant.

JOHANNES BOJESEN Commissioned by Carlsberg

MARK AIRS Commissioned by Compaq Magazine

JETTE SVANE Commissioned by the Ministry of Education

ØYVIND AASEN Self promotion

ANNE METTE EDELTOFT Commissioned for a magazine article

THOMAS BALLE Self promotion

RASMUS BREGNHØI Commissioned for a magazine article

JEANETTE BRANDT Self promotion

NYGÅRDS MARIA Commissioned by a Swedish fashion store

ERIK NIELSEN Commissioned by Danish State Railways

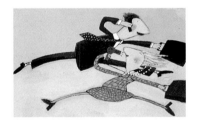

DORTHE MAILIL Commissioned by IKEA

OTTO DICKMEISS Commissioned by Euroman Magazine

TORIL BÆKMARK Commissioned by a jazz group

MORTEN VOIGT Commissioned by a technology magazine

THE ONLY ILLUSTRATION AGENCY IN DENMARK

Representing 14 professional illustrators. For further

information or to view individual portfolios contact Bettina

Thaisen or Janne Pedersen. Tel: + (45) 33 91 66 99

Skt. Pedersstræde 41B DK-1453 Copenhagen.

illustrationsBureauet

ÅSA JÄGERGÅRD
• • • • • • • • • • •

Äsas Firma
Box 49
824 21 Hudiksvall
Sweden
Tel: +46 650 13314
Fax: +46 650 13314

OVAN. Ärman en uppfinnare. Natur och Kultur, läsebok för årskurs 2. **NEDAN.** Symbol för Telekabeldivisionen, Ericsson Cables, Hudiksvall

AUGON JOHNSEN - DYNAMO BERGEN AS, TÅRNPLASS 1, N-5013 BERGEN,
TELEFON +47 55 31 22 33, TELEFAX +47 55 32 84 73,
ISDN 55328560, E-MAIL: augon@dynamo.no

UPUBLISERT

UPUBLISERT

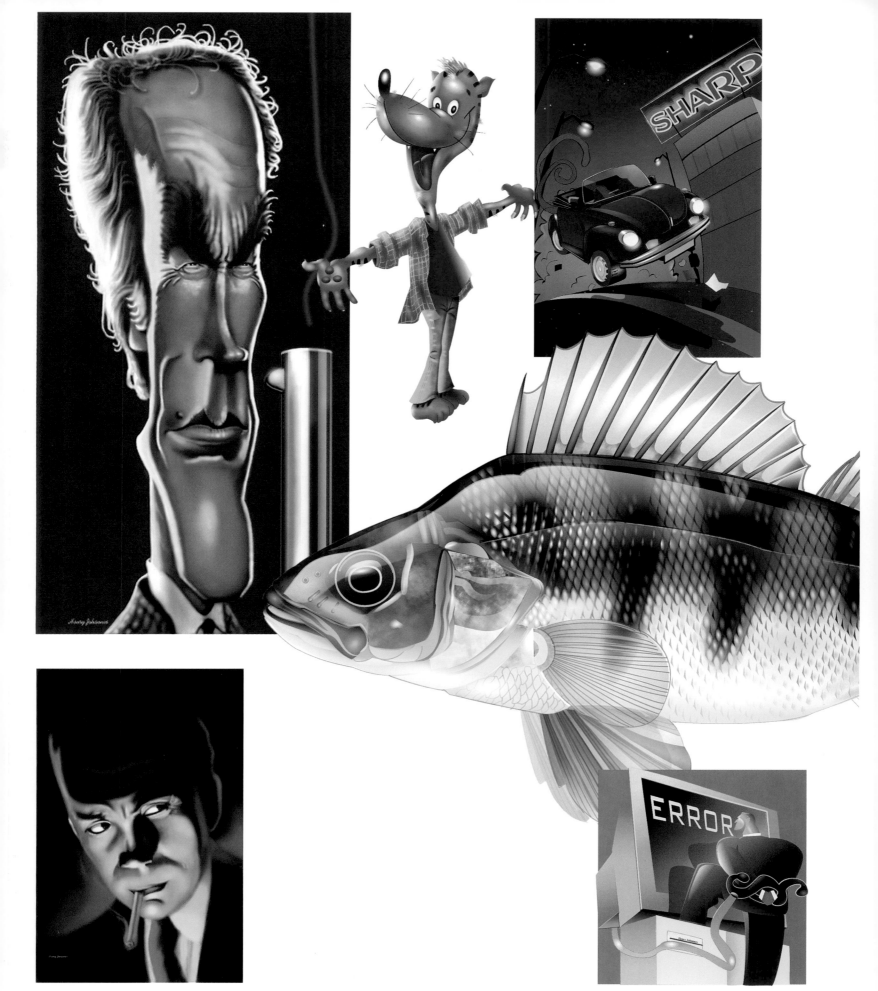

HENRY JOHANNES

Box 1242
172 25 Sundbyberg
Sweden
Tel: +46 8 291190
Fax: +46 8 982628

INGELA JONDELL

Ribegatarn 55
164 45 Kista
Sweden
Tel: +46 8 7511402

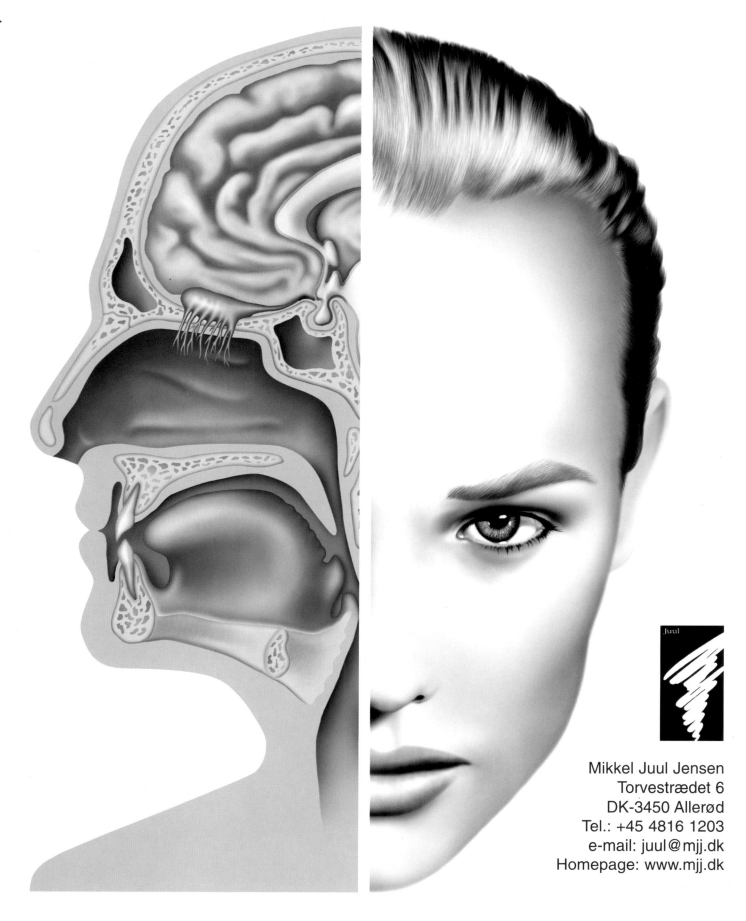

Mikkel Juul Jensen
Torvestrædet 6
DK-3450 Allerød
Tel.: +45 4816 1203
e-mail: juul@mjj.dk
Homepage: www.mjj.dk

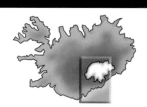

SIGRUN SÆBØ KAPSBERGER

●●●●●●●●●●●

Arbeid: Skuteviksveien 48, 5035 Bergen-Sandviken
Tel: +47 55 316620
Fax: +47 55 320081
Privat: Storevaden 22, 5084 Tertnes, Norway
Tel: +47 55 182595

Illustasjoner til eventyret "Dukken i gresset" av Asbjørnsen og Moe. N. W. Damm Forlag 1995. Gouache.

Mejeriet

M a r i e - L o u i s e
K i l e n

Grafisk design

Alle former for illustrationer
med pen og blæk
eller som computergrafik.

Mejeriet
Bøgetvej 58, Utterslev
4913 Horslunde
Telefon 53 93 60 31
Fax   53 93 60 31

Ola LINDAHL

Ynglingavägen 7
S-182 62 Djursholm
Tel   + 46 8 753 20 33
Fax   + 46 8 755 97 31
E-mail   Ola.Lindahl@mailbcx.swipnet.se
Homepage   **http://home5.swipnet.se/~w-56588**

SPACE HELPERS
an animated tv-series

SPACE HELPERS
an animated tv-series

SPACE HELPERS
an animated tv-series

BO LUNDWALL
• • • • • • • • • • • •

Wildlife art,
illustration and exhibitions

Studio: Hultsfreds Gård
S-577 36 Hultsfred
Sweden
Tel/Fax: +46 495 106 72

Studio: Birkvägen 14
S-131 40 Nacka Sweden
Tel/Fax: +46 8 718 52 09

Techniques:
Oil, watercolour and lithographs

BO LUNDWALL
● ● ● ● ● ● ● ● ● ● ● ●

Wildlife art,
illustration and exhibitions

Studio: Hultsfreds Gård
S-577 36 Hultsfred
Sweden
Tel/Fax: +46 495 106 72

Studio: Birkvägen 14
S-131 40 Nacka Sweden
Tel/Fax: +46 8 718 52 09

Techniques:
Oil, watercolour and lithographs

LARS MELANDER
• • • • • • • • • • • •

Ibsengatan 37-39
16847 Bromma
Sweden
Tel: +46 8 87 16 70

Att bygga ett företag

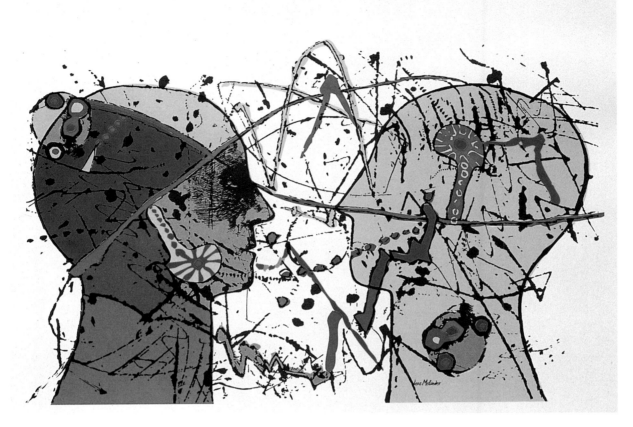

TITTEL: DEL AV KALENDER FOR MANPOWER

TITTEL: EGNE VISITTKORT MEDIA: LINOSNITT

ELISABETH MOSENG

Pilestredet 27
0164 Oslo
Norway
Tel: +47 22 11 17 90
Fax: +47 22 11 18 14

1

KJERSTI LOFTHAUG
● ● ● ● ● ● ● ● ● ● ●

Basta
Thv. Meyers Gate 56
0552 Oslo, Norway
Privat tel/faks: +47 22 351111

Vinetikett for Wittusen og Jensen A/S. Tredimen. Collage

Alle praler af succes på Internettet, men der findes stadig kun een definition: At tjene penge. Det er så let. Det handler om at lade dine kunder købe dine varer og ydelser direkte på Internettet. Med en service, der er personlig og professionel -og uden problemer med levering, betaling og sikkerhed. Ganske som I plejer - blot i en „ny butik".

Om butikken bliver en succes eller en fiasko kommer an på, hvem I sætter til at indrette den.

Det er her vi kommer ind i billedet.

Oplev os på www.preform.dk eller ring til Allan Sønderskov på telefon +45 33 16 02 60.

PREFORM REKLAME

LARS RUDEBJER

• • • • • • • • • • • • •

Laurbæråsen 9
1621 Gressvik
Norway
Tel: +47 69 36 51 91
Fax: +47 69 36 51 91

Lars Rudebjer has an art teacher education and works now professionally
illustrating children's books, school books, postcards, comic strips etc.

MORTEN SÆTREN

• • • • • • • • • • • •

Bjørn Farmannsgt. 4
0271 Oslo
Norway
Tel: +47 22 54 88 41
Fax: +47 22 54 88 41 (please call first!)
Mobile: +47 91 73 73 56

Award-winning illustration in a multitude of styles and techniques, including 3D and Photoshop.
Also total concepts (graphic design/typography).

ARNE SAMUELSEN

Dörnbergerhuset
1555 Son
Norway
Tel: +47 64 958948
Fax: +47 64 958948

*Jagär illustratör och målar i traditionella tekniker. Mina specialområden är:
Affischer, skyltställ, för packningar och digital 3D animation.*

SVANTE SEGELSON

- - - - - - - - - - -

XL Studio
Lumavägen 6, Hus 1A
120 31 Stockholm
Sweden
Tel: +46 8 6426952
Fax: +46 8 6404494
e-mail: zvante@ebox.thinet.se

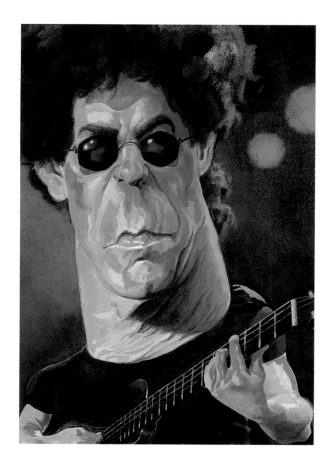

CRAIG STEPHENS
●●●●●●●●●●●●●●

Tegnestuen
St. Kongensgade 110
Copenhagen
1264 Denmark
Tel: +45 33 12 0031
Book and magazine illustrations, caricatures and cartoons.

Trelleborg AB

Illustratör

HARRIET STÅHLBERG

Fersens väg 9, S-211 42 Malmö
Tel +46 (0)40-30 79 79
Fax +46 (0)40-12 60 59

CPC Foods

Sydkraft

Findus

Frans

FRANS THEIS JENSEN

4 logos:
Photographer Ole Raffel,
Designer Thomas Cenius,
Sound Studio Ministi,
Furniture design Jannik Larsen.

Sortedam Dossering 89
2100 Copenhagen
Denmark
Tel: +45 35 26 8891
Fax: +45 35 26 8858

Clients include:
DDB Needham, DMB&B,
Saatchi & Saatchi, Ted Bates,
Ogilvy & Mather,
Young & Rubicam

CARSTEN MADSEN Tel: +38 88 10 58 / Fax: +38 88 10 58

BIRGITTE AHLMANN Tel: +38 19 72 99 / Fax: +38 88 10 58

UNDERGROUND ILLUSTRATION

● ● ● ● ● ● ● ● ● ● ● ● ●

Holger Danskes Vej 83 kld
2000 Frederiksberg
Denmark

SYDSVENSKA DAGBLADET. Sommarkampanj, helsidor dagspress. Byrå, McCann Malmö.

CITY CARD. Eget kort.

AMUHADAR. Företagspresentation, presentationsmaterial.

AMNESTY. Vykortserie.

CECILIA WAXBERG
• • • • • • • • • • • • •

RABÉN & SJÖGREN. Bild ur boken "Kan man beställa en bror". Av Dan Dan Höjer. Kommer på våren 1997.

BOEL WERNER

Hildas Stuga 9004, 771 94 Ludvika, Sweden
Tel: +46 240 17458 Fax: +46 240 15489
e-mail: per.boel@mbox301.swipnet.se

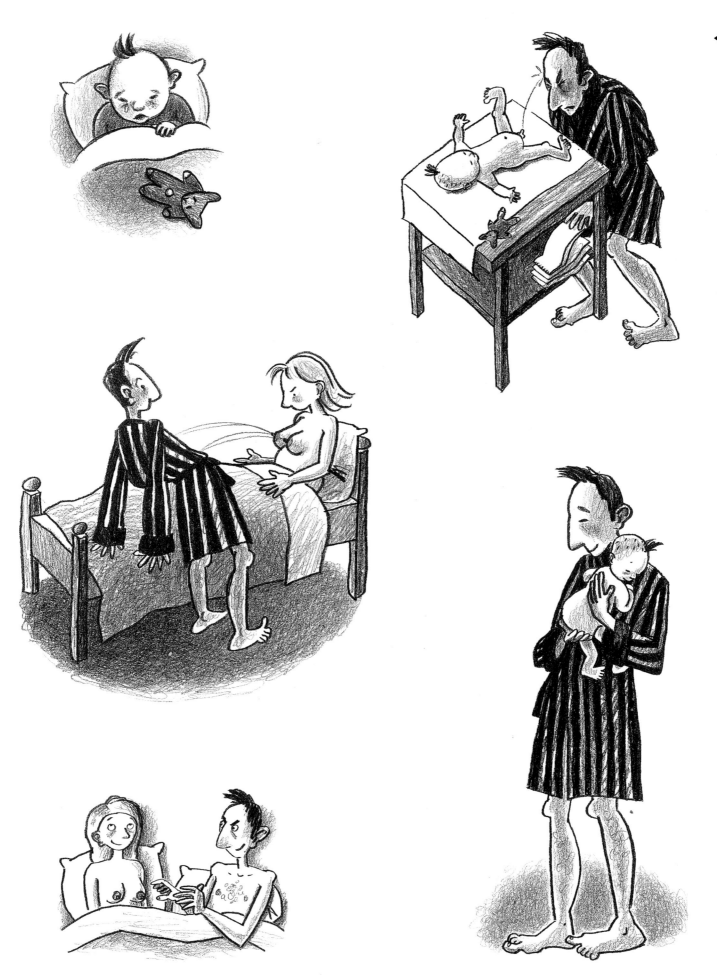

LL-FÖRLAGET 1995. Bilder ur boken "Älskade Kalle". Av Johan Werkmäster.

ELLEN WILHELMSEN
• • • • • • • • • • • •

Bestumveien 84 N
0283 Oslo
Norway
Tel: +47 22 502975
Jobb: +47 22 459830
Fax: +47 22 457660

1. Min pakistanske vert. Upublisert Tusjlavering.

Pakistansk hushjelp. Upublisert. Tusjakvarell.

MARIE ÅHFELDT
– – – – – – – – – – –

Mås Illustra
Häggviksvägen 6B
191 50 Sollentuna
Sweden
Tel: +46 8 356809

INGEFÄRA

Äter man syltad ingefära kan man känna hur det värmer i magen

Kryddaromen består av gingeroler

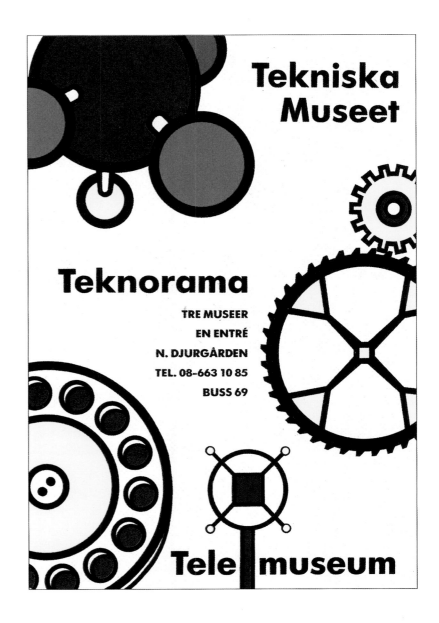

Tekniska Museet

Teknorama

TRE MUSEER
EN ENTRÉ
N. DJURGÅRDEN
TEL. 08-663 10 85
BUSS 69

Tele museum

ETHEL ÅVALL

Ethel Åvall Design
Krokusvägen 4
430 91 Hönö
Sweden
Tel: +46 31 96 92 13
Tel: +46 31 96 61 54
Fax: +46 31 96 61 54

JIMMY ALMÉN
• • • • • • • • • • • •

Alströmergatan 16
112 47 Stockholm
Sweden
Tel: +46 8 4299154
Fax: +46 8 4299154
E-mail: jimmy.almen@swipnet.se

BO FURUGREN

Bok, Bild & Text, Box 9, 230 53 Alnarp, Sweden. Tel: +46 40 462813 Fax: +46 40 461403

LOTTA GLAVE

Holländargatan 40
113 59 Stockholm
Sweden
Tel: Arbete +46 8 6606515
Tel: Bostad +46 8 329898
Fax: Arbete +46 8 6641573
Fax: Bostad +46 8 329898

CHRISTINE GÖHLNER

● ● ● ● ● ● ● ● ● ● ● ●

Drömverksta'n
Box 4157
400 40 Göteborg, Sweden
Tel: +46 10 2345645

FÖRSTAMAJBLOMMANS RIKSFÖRBUND. Julkort på temat "Göteborg vid sekelskiftet".

THOMAZ GRAHL
- - - - - - - - - - - - - - -

Grahlstänk AB, Rådhusgatan,
3 Box 26, 733 21 Sala Sweden.
Tel: +46 224 87097
Fax: +46 224 15753

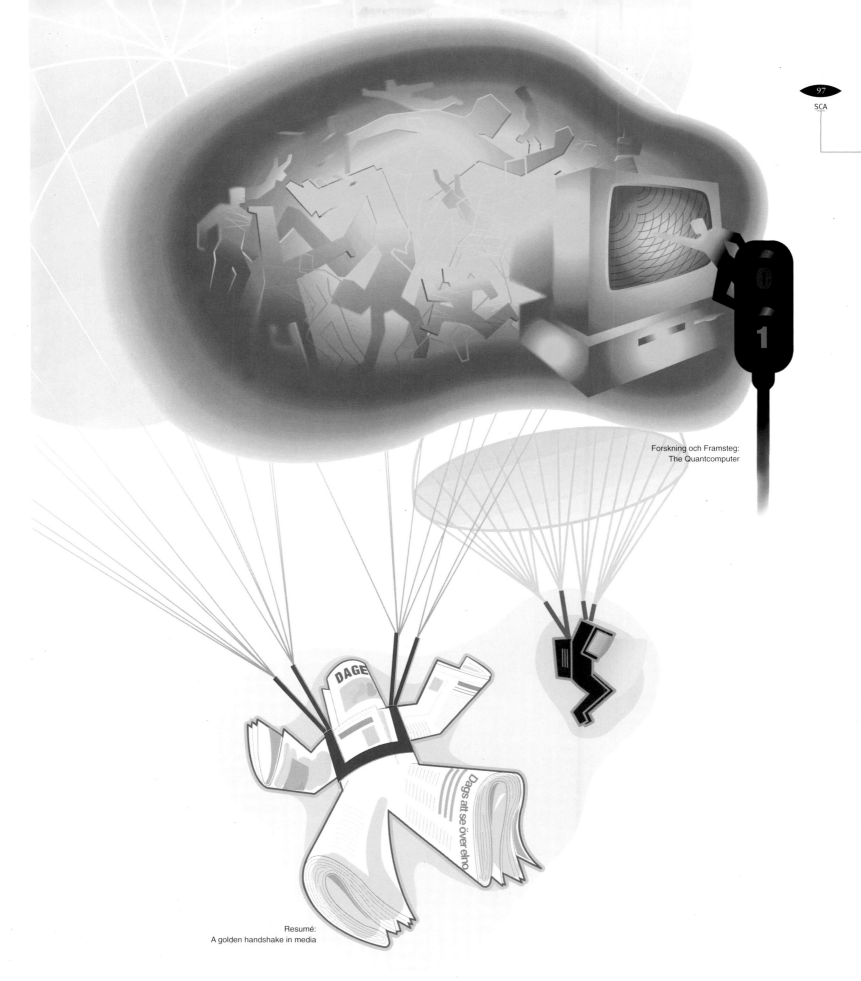

Forskning och Framsteg:
The Quantcomputer

Resumé:
A golden handshake in media

ILLUSTRA ILISTE

Airi Iliste
Olof Gjödingsgatan 5
112 31 Stockholm
airi@swipnet.se
☎ 46 8 653 56 89

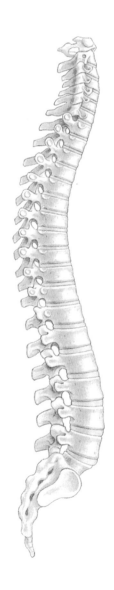

ROLAND KLANG

● ● ● ● ● ● ● ● ● ● ●

Roland Klang AB
Molkomsbacken 26
123 33 Farsta
Sweden
Tel: +46 8 6043409
Tel: +46 8 50156189
Fax: +46 8 6043409

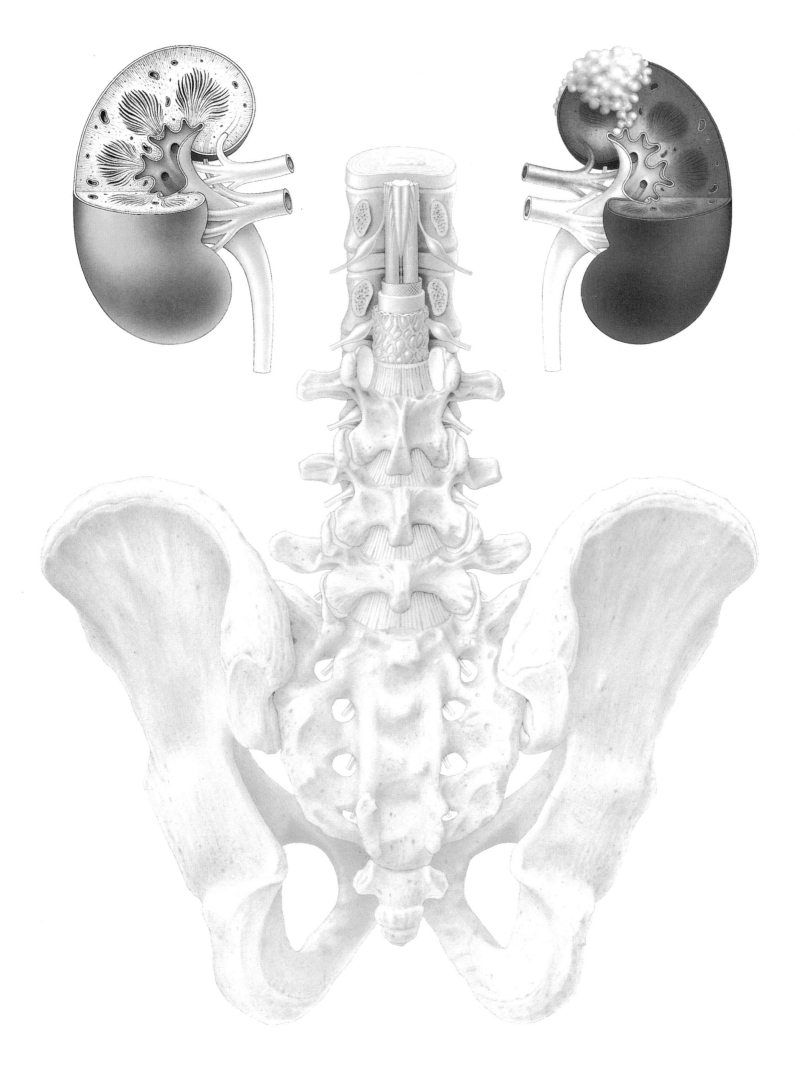

Roland Klang works mainly with medical and scientific illustrations, paintings, wooden sculptures and graphic arts.

KAJSA LINDH
• • • • • • • • • • • •

Kajsas Tecknarstuga, c/o Kajsa Lindh, Berghagsvägen 9A, 660 40 Skåpafors, Sweden. Tel: +46 531 42085

1.

2.

3.

4.

6.

LOTTA PERSSON

• • • • • • • • • • • • •

Lotta Persson Firma
Banehagsgatan 1E
414 51 Göteborg
Sweden
Tel: +46 31 424143
Fax: +46 31 143602

OLLE QVENNERSTEDT

Olle Qvennerstedt Illustration AB, Smågården, Blacksta, 646 91 Gnesta, Sweden. Tel: +46 158 30340 Fax: +46 158 30360

PHARMACIA. Kampanj för ACO, Byrå, Heart, Stefan Olsson.

POUTTU. Korvförpackningar, Byrå, Agency/Söderberg.

LANDSTINGET. Byrå, Christensen & Karlsson.

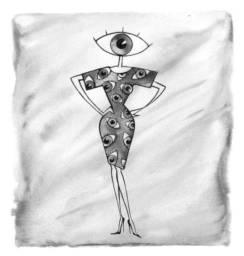

SVERIGES KONTAKTLINSFÖRENING. Byrå, Christensen & Karlsson.

GUNILLA SCHELIN

Schelin Illustrationer AB
Baggensg. 17
111 31 Stockholm
Sweden
Tel: +46 8 101881
Fax: +46 8 102182

ACO. Annonser. Byrå, Lybergs.

INGA-STINA RÖNNE
• • • • • • • • • • • •

Inga-Stina Rönne Illustration, Dalagatan 44, 113 24 Stockholm, Sweden. Tel: +46 8 329923 Fax: +46 8 329923

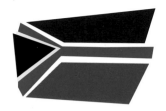

SOUTH AFRICA

ILLUSTRATION

Martha Helen Knowles

· · · · · · · · · ·

53 17th street
Orange Grove
2192
Tel: (2711) 485 3990
E-mail address: marthaknowles@hotmail.com

Robyn Jephson

· · · · · · · · · ·

85 12th Street
Parkhurst
2193
Tel: (2711) 788 6625

Harry Penberthy

· · · · · · · · · ·

P.O. Box 77167
Fontainbleau
2032
Tel: (2711) 793 1924

S P A I N
E S P A Ñ A

I L L U S T R A T I O N
I L U S T R A C I Ó N

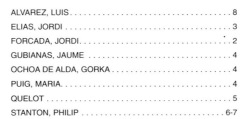

IL·LUSTRACIÓ / DISSENY GRÀFIC / PACKAGING

JORDI FORCADA

C/ SANT TOMÀS, 52 BAIXOS
08032 BARCELONA
TELEF/FAX. +3 43 3576618

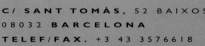

"LA CAIXA"

PROMOCIONAL

SKONTER

CASA COSTA

SALADE MELANGEE
de Jeunes Pousses

UP TO DATE

EL PERIODICO DE CATALUNYA

GUARRO CASAS

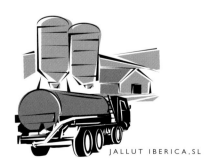

JALLUT IBERICA, SL

jordi Elias

DR. A. PUJADAS 10 EB A2. 08830 SANT BOI. BCN. TEL-FAX 630 79 30.
Email; jelias@idgrup.ibernet.com

GORKA OCHOA DE ALDA
C/ Domingo Beltran 4, 5º
01012 Barcelona
Tel / Fax: 945-141 775

MARIA PUIG
Casanova 105,pral.1ª
08036 Barcelona
Tel / Fax: 93-451 83 56
Editorial, Comic

JAUME GUBIANAS
C/ Anselm Clavé nº 2
08670 Navàs (Barcelona)
Tel / Fax: 93-839 07 06
e-mail: gubianas@seker.es
http://bbs.seker.es/~gubianas

OVELOT

IL·LUSTRACIÓ
C/ Cingles, 33
08211 Sant Feliu del Racó
Barcelona (Spain)
Tel. i Fax (93) 714 49 11

ES

Ilustración de Barcelona con motivo de la boda de Cristina de Borbón e Iñaki Urdangarin para
la revista Magazine de la Vanguardia, portada

Stanton Studio s.l.

Avión Plus Ultra 35   tel (93) 205 44 19   fax 205 72 76

Barcelona 08017   e-mail:stanton@seker.es

Ilustración contra el racismo para la revista Nexus
de la Fundació Caixa de Catalunya

ideas e imágenes

para editoriales, agencias de publicidad, estudios de diseño gráfico,
televisiones, textiles, espacios efímeros (teatro y escaparates).

ideas and images for editorial, advertising, graphic design, television, textile, theatre and window design.

LUIS ALVAREZ
TEL/FAX.218 62 10
SANTA PERPETUA,14 ENT
08012-BARCELONA

Inhaltsverzeichnis

UNITED KINGDOM

ILLUSTRATION

MIDLANDS & N

one

one

one

one

one

ROB HEFFERAN

17 St Stephens Road
Penketh
Warrington
Cheshire WA5 2AN
Tel: +44 (0)1925 728802
Fax: +44 (0)1925 791411

Working with acrylics, I produce work for advertising agencies, book publishers and various magazines. Please ring for an extensive set of samples.

ROB HEFFERAN
• • • • • • • • • • • •

17 St Stephens Road
Penketh
Warrington
Cheshire WA5 2AN
Tel: +44 (0)1925 728802
Fax: +44 (0)1925 791411

Working with acrylics, I produce work for advertising agencies, book publishers and various magazines. Please ring for an extensive set of samples.

ARLENE ADAMS
· · · · · · · · · · · ·

114 Springfield Road
Kings Heath
Birmingham B14 7DY
Tel/Fax: +44 (0)121 441 5829

Agent: Which Art, Kurgartenweg 4,
D-59556 Bad Waldliesborn, Germany
Tel: 02941 8320   Fax: 02941 82210

Work also in colour

Clients include: Cadbury's, Parker Pens, Mercedez Benz,
Hewlett Packard, Renault (France), Shell UK, ICi,
Dorling Kindersley

THE APPLE AGENCY

No. 4 Skippingdale Business Park
Exmoor Avenue, Scunthorpe
N. Lincolnshire DN15 8NJ
Tel: +44 (0)1724 289081
Fax: +44 (0)1724 289381
To view 450 pages: http://www.appleagency.co.uk
Email: simonb@appleagency.co.uk

THE APPLE AGENCY

• • • • • • • • • •

No. 4 Skippingdale Business Park
Exmoor Avenue, Scunthorpe
N. Lincolnshire DN15 8NJ
Tel: +44 (0)1724 289081
Fax: +44 (0)1724 289381
To view 450 pages: http://www.appleagency.co.uk
Email: simonb@appleagency.co.uk

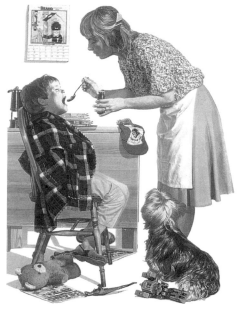

THE ART BUSINESS

22 Dennington Lane
Crigglestone, Wakefield
West Yorkshire WF4 3ET
Tel: +44 (0)1924 259 313
Fax: +44 (0)1924 240 857

THE
ART
BUSINESS
ILLUSTRATORS
AGENTS

THE ART BUSINESS

•••••••••••••

*22 Dennington Lane
Crigglestone, Wakefield
West Yorkshire WF4 3ET
Tel: +44 (0)1924 259 313
Fax: +44 (0)1924 240 857*

**THE
ART
BUSINESS**
ILLUSTRATORS
A G E N T S

two

two

SCOTLAND

two

two

two

ANDREW FOLEY
• • • • • • • • • • •

10 Mingarry Street (2/2)
Glasgow G20 8NT
Tel/Fax: +44 (0)141 946 8894

Clients include: Reader's Digest, Heinemann, Loco Foco Ltd, Quorum Design, The Glasgow Herald, The Big Issue in Scotland

eastwing

98 Columbia Road
London E2 7QB
T 0171 613 5580
F 0171 613 2726

CLARE HEWITT
• • • • • • • • • • •

Studio, 15 Meadow Place
Edinburgh EH9 1JR
Tel: +44 (0)131 229 8345

STEPHEN LEE
• • • • • • • • • • •

1 Coates Place
Edinburgh EH37 7AA
Tel: +44 (0)1307 462664

LONDON & SOUTH

three

three

three

three

CHRIS BURKE
••••••••••

17 Upper Grosvenor Road
Tunbridge Wells
Kent TN1 2DU
Tel/Fax: +44 (0)1892 531329

Clients include: Comic Relief, Creative Review, ES Magazine, F.T., Irish Tourist Board, M&S, Punch, Penguin, Pentagram, Radio Times, Sunday Times

LONDON & SOUTH

HAMZA ARCAN

The Studio
1 Salisbury Road
Hove
East Sussex
BN3 3AB
Tel: +44 (0)1273 205030
Fax: +44 (0)1273 720373

CHRIS BURKE
- - - - - - - - - - - -

17 Upper Grosvenor Road
Tunbridge Wells
Kent TN1 2DU
Tel/Fax: +44 (0)1892 531329

Clients include: Comic Relief, Creative Review, ES Magazine, F.T., Irish Tourist Board, M&S, Punch, Penguin, Pentagram, Radio Times, Sunday Times

GILL BUTTON

- - - - - - - - - - - -

Tel: +44 (0)7000 785492
Fax: +44 (0)7000 785493
Mobile: 0973 402885

Recent clients include: Sunday Times, The Independent, The Telegraph, E.S., F.T., Royal Mail, Little Brown, Reed, Premier, BBC and Condé Nast

MICHAEL CHARSLEY
• • • • • • • • • • • •

Agent:
M Robinson, 28 Clyde Road
Sutton, Surrey SM1 2RR
Tel: +44 (0)181 642 1170

17 Felbridge Close
Sutton
Surrey SM2 5QH
Home +44 (0)181 642 2922
Studio +44 (0)178 448 3045

*Innovative experienced versatile
illustrator. Specialist in highly detailed
airbrush and oil cartoons, caricatures
and classic figure work.*

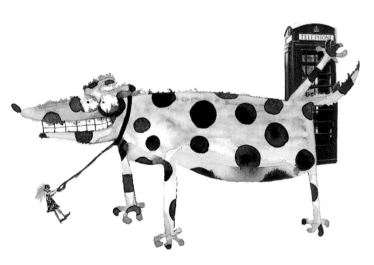

KIM COLLINS

81A Albion Road
Stoke Newington
London N16 9PL
Tel/Fax: +44 (0)171 249 7370

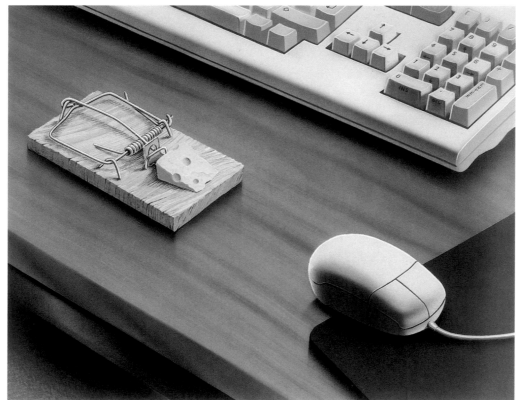

RUPERT EARL

64 Islington Road
Southville
Bristol BS3 1PZ
Tel: +44 (0)117 9631789

ADAM GRAFF

Agent: The Organisation
69 Caledonian Road
London N1 9BT
Tel: +44 (0)171 833 8268
Fax: +44 (0)171 833 8269

10 St. Columbus House
Prospect Hill
Walthamstow E17 3AZ
Tel: +44 (0)181 521 7182

*Work combines traditional drawing techniques
with computer technology to apply colour*

JAMES MEALING

ART INSTRUCTION

CRAFTS

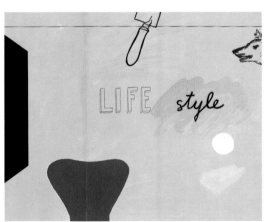

LIFE style

MARION DEUCHARS

HEART

T +44 (0)171 833 4447
F +44 (0)171 833 4446

floor 2 no1 tysoe street london EC1R 4SA

STEWART HARRIS
● ● ● ● ● ● ● ● ● ● ●

1 Harvey Goodwin Gardens
Cambridge CB4 3EZ
Tel: +44 (0)1223 364256

Cambridge-based illustrator, studied at Winchester School of Art, Chelsea College of Art and Design and Anglia Polytechnic University

SARA HAYWARD

31 Diglis Road
Worcester WR5 3BW
Tel: +44 (0)1905 357563

CHRISTIAAN IKEN

●●●●●●●●●●

21 Lorne Park Mansions
33 Lorne Park Road
Bournemouth BH1 1JL
Tel/Fax: +44 (0)1202 780432

Scenes from Cyber-punk / Fantasy comic
Specializing in Fantasy and Cyber-punk Art

Looking for publisher

CHUAN KHOO

27 Whitmore Street
Maidstone
Kent ME16 8JX
Tel/Fax: +44 (0)1622 721987

Clients include: Canon (UK) Ltd, British Alcan, United Airlines, Middlesex University, Singapore Dance Theatre

SCOTT LYDON

• • • • • • • • • • • •

136 Hansons Bridge Road
Erdington
Birmingham B24 0PB
Tel: +44 (0)121 351 3379

KRIDON PANTELI
● ● ● ● ● ● ● ● ● ● ● ● ●

Panteli Illustration
75 Mercers Road
London N19 4PS
Tel/Fax: +44 (0)171 272 9940
Pager: +44 (0)1523 169064

ARVIND SHAH

17 Daylesford Avenue
Putney
London SW15 5QR
Tel: +44 (0)181 876 2277

I am a freelance illustrator but my main field of work is
writing and illustrating children's books.

RICHARD J. SMITH

Valley Farm
Dagnall
Berkhamsted HP4 1QR
Tel: +44 (0)1442 843783

1. Fog, Frost Fox & Friend

2. Bone Fish

advertising

advertising

advertising
judges

Dennis Willison / Senior Art Director / Saatchi & Saatchi

Annie Leonard / Art Buyer / Abbot Mead Vickers

Paddy Morahan / Project Manager / Bartle Bogle Hegarty

George Martin / Art Buyer / Ammarati Puris Lintas

Mark Reddy / Illustrator

andrew bylo

38B Southwell
Road
London
SE5 9PG

t: 0171 274 4116
f: 0171 738 3743

18
GB

title
Wine Boxes

medium
Acrylic

purpose of work
Point of sale, beer
wine and spirits

brief
'Glyndebourne'-
style picnic using
bold rich warm
brushstrokes. Must
also be able to
take landscape
format section from
middle.

commissioned by
Paul Hutton

company
Safeway

Dennis Willison / Senior Art Director / Saatchi & Saatchi

Annie Leonard / Art Buyer / Abbot Mead Vickers

Paddy Morahan / Project Manager / Bartle Bogle Hegarty

George Martin / Art Buyer / Ammarati Puris Lintas

Mark Reddy / Illustrator

james marsh

21 Elms Road
London
SW4 9ER

t: 0171 622 9530
f: 0171 498 6851

16
GB

title
La Bohème

medium
Acrylic on canvas

purpose of work
Posters and
brochures

brief
One in a set of six
paintings for
1997/98 Opera
Season

commissioned by
Heidi Bornstein

company
Seattle Opera

bill greenhead

1 Vicarage Crescent
London
SW11 3LP

t: 0171 228 8882

title
Tuff

medium
Pentel pens and
mechanical spot
colour

purpose of work
Comic cover for
Levi's

brief
Risqué comic cover
for the Levi's Mr
Boombastic
Campagin

commisioned by
Glenn

company
Tango/BBH

agent
Illustration
1 Vicarage Crescent
London
SW11 3LP
t: 0171 228 8882

andrew bylo

38B Southwell
Road
London
SE5 9PG

t: 0171 274 4116
f: 0171 738 3743

title
Wine Boxes

medium
Acrylic

purpose of work
Point of sale, beer
wine and spirits

brief
'Glyndebourne'-
style picnic using
bold rich warm
brushstrokes. Must
also be able to
take landscape
format section from
middle.

commissioned by
Paul Hutton

company
Safeway

andrew bylo

38B Southwell
Road
London
SE5 9PG

t: 0171 274 4116
f: 0171 738 3743

19

GB

title
Spain, Portugal and
Italy

medium
Acrylic

purpose of work
Point of sale for
beer, wines and
spirits

brief
Evoke mood and
feeling of country
of origin using bold
rich warm
brushstrokes. Must
be able to take
landscape format
section from
middle

commissioned by
Paul Hutton

company
Safeway

MAGNET
ARTISTS

sue climpson

1 Vicarage Crescent
London
SW11 3LP

☆ *images 22* exhibitor

t: 0171 228 8882/8886

title
Kenco Coffee - 1

medium
Photoshop, live
picture,
photography and
art work

purpose of work
Advertisement

brief
Kenco - given
outline requirement

commissioned by
Chris Mattey

company
Kenco Coffee

Agent
Illustration
1 Vicarage Crescent
London
SW11 3LP
t: 0171 228 8882

sue climpson

1 Vicarage Crescent
London
SW11 3LP

t: 0171 228 8882

title
Kenco Coffee - 2
medium
Photoshop, live
picture,
photography and
art work
purpose of work
Advertising

brief
Kenco - given
outline requirement
commissioned by
Chris Mattey
company
Kenco Coffee
agent
Illustration
1 Vicarage Crescent
London
SW11 3LP
t: 0171 228
8882/8886

adrian hardy

3 Vernon Road
Turnpike Lane
London N8 0QD

t: 0181 888 5275

22
GB

title
La Tomatina

medium
Hand Montage

purpose of work
Advertising

brief
To advertise
Gonzalez Byass
Sherry. English man
(Hugh Laurie type)
abroad at the
tomato throwing
festival, Valencia

commissioned by
Gonzalez Byass

company
Simons Palmer

matilda harrison

c/- Arena
144 Royal College
Street
London
NW1 0TA

t: 0171 267 9661
f: 0171 284 0486

GB

title
Dog

medium
Acrylic

purpose of work
Press advertising
campaign for
Purina Pro Plan

brief
To promote a
healthy dog who's
fed on Pro-Plan
dog food

commissioned by
Lindsey Winton

company
Saatchi & Saatchi

agent
Arena
144 Royal College
Street
London
NW1 0TA
t: 0171 267 9661

paul hess

1 Vicarage Crescent
London

☆ *images 22* exhibitor

children's books

children's books
judges

Chris Inns / Deputy Art Director / Penguin Children's Books

Sarah Hodder / Art Director / Orchard Books

Judith Elliott / Director / Orion Children's Books

Stephen Cartwright / Illustrator

Mike Watts / Deputy Art Director, Fiction / Harper Collins Children's Books

andrew davidson

Moors Cottage
Swells Hill
Burleigh
Stroud
GL5 2SP

t: 01483 884 650
f: 01453 887 012

★ children's books section winner
★ winner: *The Transworld Children's Book Award*
☆ *images 22* exhibitor

38
GB

title
Godhanger Series
medium
Wood engraving
purpose of work
Children's book
illustration

brief
Illustrate a passage
in Dick King-
Smith's book
Godhanger, a
symbolically
religious narrative
commissioned by
Ian Butterworth
company
Transworld
Publishing
agent
The Artworks
70 Rosaline Road
London SW16 7RT
t: 0171 610 1801

alex ayliffe

86 High Street
Codicote
Herts S94 8XE

t: 01438 821446

title
Oh No, Anna!

medium
Paper collage

purpose of work
to provide a
concept about
colours for pre-
school children

brief
To illustrate a
picture book with
flaps

commissioned by
Levinson Children's
Books

tiphanie beeke

24 Northview Road
New Costessey
Norwich
Norfolk NR5 0BG

t: 01603 744588

title
The Brand New
Creature

medium
Watercolour and
acrylic

purpose of work
Illustrations for
children's picture
book

brief
To illustrate a
children's picture
book about
searching for a
crocodile and
capturing the heat,
colour and wildlife
of Africa

commissioned by
Tiffany Leeson

company
Levinson Children's
Books

derek brazell

28 Hatton House
Hindmarsh Close
London
E1 8JH

t: 0171 265 1896
f: 0171 265 1896

title
Pig-Heart Boy

medium
Pencil and
Watercolour

purpose of work
Book cover

brief
To choose an
image from the
book that would
make an eye-
catching cover

commissioned by
Peter Bennett

company
Transworld
Publishers

agent
Artist Partners
14-18 Ham Yard
Great Windmill
Street
London W1V 8DE
t: 0171 734 7991
f: 0171 287 0371

frances cony

21 Tyndalls Park
Road
Bristol
BS8 1PQ

t: 0117 973 0022
f: 0117 973 0022

44
GB

title
A Blushing Zebra!

medium
Pen and ink and
watercolour

purpose of work
Children's flap-
book illustration

brief
To answer the joke
'What's black and
white and red all
over?' - the
question being
printed on a
shower curtain flap
in *Zebra Jokes*
book

commissioned by
Sheri Safran

company
Sadie Fields
Productions Ltd

client
Tango Books

allan drummond

The White House
High Street
Dedham
CO7 6HL

t: 01206 322 360
f: 01206 322 360

45

GB

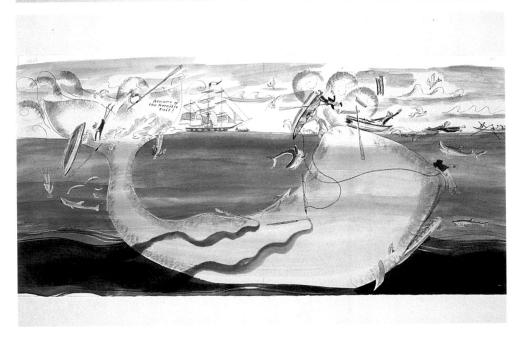

title
Moby Dick
medium
pen, watercolour
purpose
Cover and
illustrations for
children's book
brief
Illustrations to the
artist's own
adaptation of *Moby
Dick* for children,
written, designed
and illustrated by
the artist
commissioned by
Francesca Dow
company
Orchard Books

sara fanelli

Flat 11
Howitt Close
Howitt Road
London NW3 4LX

t: 0171 483 2544
f: 0171 483 2544

46
GB

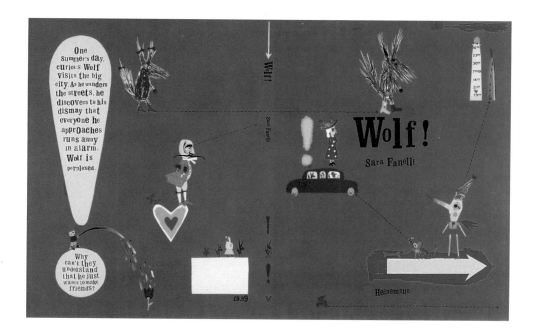

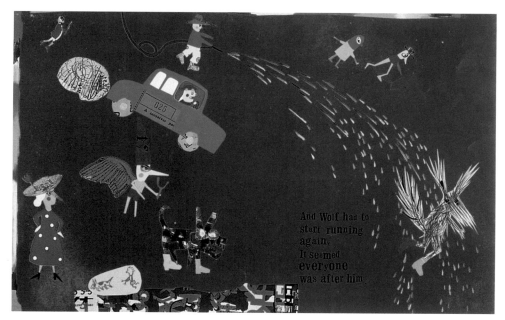

title
Wolf!

medium
Collage

purpose
Children's book

brief
Children's book

commissioned by
Heinemann

company
Reed Books

teresa flavin

Wellpark Enterprise
Centre
120 Sydney Street
Glasgow
G31 1JF

t: 0141 550 4994
f: 0141 550 4443

title
Tomkin Opens the
Rainclouds

medium
Acrylic on paper

purpose of work
Illustration for a
fairy tale

brief
Illustration for
*Tomkin and the
Three-Legged Stool*
by Vivian French
for the anthology
*Classic Fairy Tales
to Read Aloud*

commissioned by
Caroline Johnson

company
Kingfisher Books

agent
Publisher 's
Graphics (North
America only)
251 Greenwood Ave
Bethel, CT 06801
USA
t: (203) 797 8188

adrian reynolds

86 Chesterton Road
Cambridge
CB4 1ER

☆ *images 22* exhibitor

58

editorial

Deborah George / Art Editor / *New Scientist* Magazine

Colin McHenry / Group Art Director / *Creative Review*

Anne Braybon / Art Director / *Rx* Magazine

Anne Morrow / Illustration Editor / *Weekend Guardian*

Peter Till / Illustrator

david hughes

Rosemount Studios
43 Station Road
Marple
SK6 6AJ

t: 0161 427 3852
f: 0161 427 8100

60
GB

★ editorial section winner
★ winner: *The Pentagram Award*
☆ *images 22* exhibitor

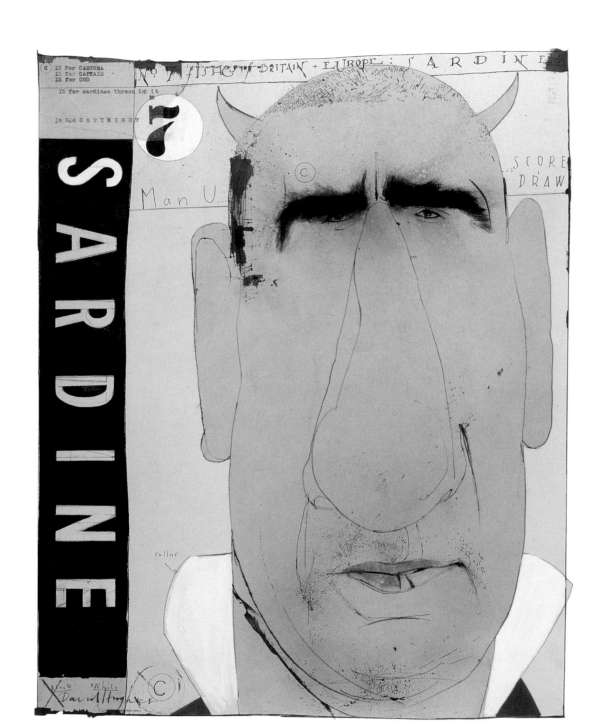

title
Eric Cantona
medium
Pen and ink,
watercolour,
charcoal and
gouache
purpose of work
Full-page
illustration for *The
Times* Magazine

brief
A portrait of Eric
Cantona
commissioned by
David Curless
client
The Times

paul blow

Flat 4
68 St Aubyns
Hove
BN3 2TE

℡: 01273 779737
f: 01273 779 737

GB

title
Passing Off
medium
Acrylic
purpose of work
Editorial

brief
Illustrate the
problem of
companies using
well-known trade
names to pass off
their own products

commissioned by
Steve Aylett

commissioned by
New Law Journal

stuart briers

33 Eswyn Road
Tooting
London
SW17 8TR

t: 0181 767 2618

62
GB

christopher gilvan-cartwright

36 Wellington Street
London WC2E 7BD

t: 0171 240 8925
f: 0171 836 1177

64
GB

title
The Great Escape:
Commuter's Guide
to the Southwest
medium
Acrylic
purpose of work
Cover in a series of
six weekly
commuter guides

brief
Aspirational view
evoking the South-
West commuter
belt
commissioned by
Anne Braybon
company
Sunday Telegraph
agent
The Central
Illustration Agency
36 Wellington
Street London
WC2E 7BD
t: 0171 240 8925

jovan djordjevic

9 Fairlop Road
London
E11 1BL

t: 0181 539 3892
f: 0181 539 3893

65

GB

title
Different for Girls

medium
Montage and ink

purpose of work
Editorial - money
matters in *The
Observer*

brief
Unlike gay men,
lesbians who come
out still face
enormous
hostilities at work

company
The Observer

emma dodd

Black Hat Studio
4 Northington
Street
Bloomsbury
London
WC1N 2JG

t: 0171 430 9163
f: 0171 430 9156

☆ *images 22* exhibitor

66

GB

title
Scientist and
Fingerprint
medium
Illustrator software
purpose of work
News story in
Gardener's World
Magazine
brief
Article about
counteracting the
trade in fake plants
by identifying
individual plant
cells, similar to
police use of DNA
fingerprinting

commissioned by
Abigail Dodd
company
BBC Gardener's
World
agent
Dave Morrison
Black Hat Studio
4 Northington Street
Bloomsbury
London WC1N 2JG
t: 0171 430 9146

8 Elfin Lodge
Elfin Grove
Teddington
TW11 8RE

t: 0976 242 378
t/f: 0181 977 8924

67

GB

title
Every Body Hurts
medium
Digital sampling
montage
purpose of work
To accompany an
article

brief
illustrate a feature
on back injury in
the music biz
(specifically
guitarists)
commissioned by
Tony Horkins
company
IPC
client
Melody Maker

simon fell

87 Rothschild Road
London
W4 5NT

t: 0181 994 6206
f: 0181 994 6206

68

GB

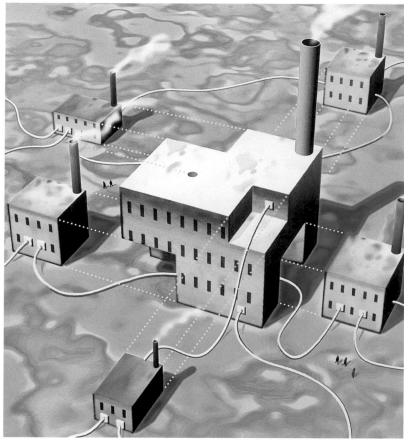

title
The Year 2000 and
the Internet
medium
Colour copy and
acrylic
purpose of work
Magazine
illustration

brief
Problems caused
by computer
software that does
not recognise the
turn of the century
could be
transmitted across
the internet
commissioned by
K Falconer
company
Network Reseller
client
Dennis Publishing

title
Contracting Out
medium
Computer
generated (Bryce
2.0 and Photoshop
3.0)
purpose of work
Magazine article

brief
Companies are
finding it is more
efficient to contract
out large parts of
their
administration,
leaving them to
concentrate on
their core business
commissioned by
Gene Cornelius
company
The Engineer
client
Miller Freeman
Technical

jason ford

c/- Heart
2nd Floor,
1 Tysoe Street
_ondon
EC1R 4SA

t: 0171 833 4447

69
GB

title
The Emerald Affair
medium
Acrylic and ink
purpose of work
Illustration for
Radio 2 programme

brief
"I saw him as a
symptom of the
age...a man always
out to make a
profit."
commissioned by
Matthew Bookman
company
Radio Times
agent
Heart
2nd Floor
1 Tysoe Street
London
EC1R 4SA
t: 0171 833 4447

geoff grandfield

30 Allen Road
London
N16 8SA

t: 0171 241 1523

title
Rural Ride
medium
Pastel
purpose of work
Illustrate weekly
column on rural life

brief
Respond to
narrative on rural
burglary, Film Noir
mood
commissioned by
Anne Braybon
company
*The Sunday
Telegraph*

brian grimwood

36 Wellington St
London
WC2E 7BD

℡: 0171 240 8925
⊹: 0171 836 1177

title
John Galliano
medium
Gouache
purpose of work
*The Sunday
Telegraph
Magazine*

brief
Saint or sinner
section
commissioned by
Anne Braybon
company
*The Sunday
Telegraph
Magazine*
agent
CIA
36 Wellington
Street
London
WC2E 7BD
t: 0171 240 8925
e.mail: c.illustration
a@dail.pipex.com

brian grimwood

36 Wellington St
London
WC2E 7BD

t: 0171 240 8925
f: 0171 836 1177

title
The Last Word

medium
Gouache

purpose of work
Editorial

brief
Illustrate the article

commissioned by
John Belknap

company
The Express

agent
CIA
36 Wellington Street
London
WC2E 7BD
t: 0171 240 8925
e.mail:
c.illustrationa@dail.pipex.com

brian grimwood

36 Wellington St
London
WC2E 7BD

t: 0171 240 8925
f: 0171 836 1177

73

GB

title
Words and Music

medium
Gouache

purpose of work
Editorial

brief
To enhance the
front cover of *The
Guardian Review*

commissioned by
Simon Esterson,
Roger Browning

company
The Guardian

agent
36 Wellington Street
London
WC2E 7BD
0171 240 8925
e.mail:
c.illustrationa@dail.pipex.com

george hardie

Drounces
White Chimney
Row
Westbourne
Emsworth
PO10 8RS

t: 01243 377 528
f: 01243 370 769

74
GB

★ **award winner:** *The Pentagram Award*
☆ *images 22* exhibitor

title
Umberto Verdi,
Chimney Sweep

medium
Ink and Xerox on
to coloured papers

purpose of work
Illustration for
Radio 4 play

brief
A bored and lonely
mum chooses the
most romantic
name when her
chimney needs
cleaning. Will
Umberto's Latin
touch sweep her
off her feet?

commissioned by
Nathan Gale

company
Radio Times

matilda harrison

c/- Arena
144 Royal College
Street
London
NW1 0TA

t: 0171 267 9661
f: 0171 284 0486

title
Castles in the Sand
medium
Acrylic

purpose of work
Full-page editorial
illustration for *The
Independent*
Magazine

brief
Fading love turns a
long-married
couple into
strangers on the
shore: extract from
a novel by Amy
Bloom
commissioned by
Gary Cochrane

company
The Independent

agent
Arena
144 Royal College
Street
London
NW1 0TH
t: 0171 267 9661

robert heesom

Wyatts
Rectory Drive
Bidborough
Tunbridge Wells
TN3 0UL

t: 01892 549084
f: 01892 549084

title
Networking

medium
Acrylic on canvas

purpose of work
To illustrate an article in *PC Magazine*

brief
How information can be passed around computer networks. The extra 'flying' hands denote unseen eavesdroppers grabbing the information

commissioned by
Hazel Bennington

company
Ziff-Davis UK Limited

client
PC Magazine

title
Pass the Parcel

medium
Acrylic on canvas

purpose of work
To illustrate an article in *PC Magazine*

brief
ISDN 'routers' are used to send computer information to the right destination. Here a postman re-routes the packets of information

commissioned by
Hazel Bennington

company
Ziff-Davis UK Ltd

client
PC Magazine

angela j hogg

56 Astbury Road
London
SE15 2NJ

t: 0171 732 5957

title
100th anniversary
of the electron

medium
Acrylic and collage

purpose of work
To illustrate a
magazine article

brief
To illustrate an
article about the
history past and
present of the
electron particle

commissioned by
New Scientist

agent
The Inkshed
98 Columbia Road
London
E2 7QB
t: 0171 613 2323

ciaran hughes

33 Reservoir Road
London
SE4 2NU

t: 0171 771 0615
f: 0171 771 0615
e.mail: thebhoys@dircon.co.uk

80
GB

title
The Eye of the
Beholder

medium
Adobe Photoshop

purpose of work
Accompany article
on judging
competitions in a
magazine

brief
Show what it's like
to judge and be
judged in
competitions

commissioned by
Brendan Foley

company
Foley Associates

client
Communicators in
Business

satoshi kambayashi

Flat 2
40 Tisbury Road
Hove
East Sussex
BN3 3BA
t: 01273 771539
f: 01273 771539
pager: 01426 131519

title
The Nowhere Man
in Transit Lounge

medium
India ink and
watercolour

purpose of work
Editorial illustration
for *Prospect*
Magazine

brief
To illustrate an
essay by Pico Iyer
about the new
transcontinental
people for whom
home is everywhere
and nowhere

commissioned by
Susan Buchanan

company
Buchanan-Davey

client
Prospect Magazine

agent
Ian Fleming and
Associates
72-74 Brewer
Street, London
W1R 3PH
t: 0171 734 8701

satoshi kambayashi

Flat 2
40 Tisbury Road
Hove
East Sussex
BN3 3BA
t: 01273 771539
f: 01273 771539
pager: 01426 131519

title
Treasure Trove

medium
India ink and
watercolour

purpose of work
Cover illustration
for *New Law
Journal*

brief
To produce a cover
illustration featuring
the article reviewing
the new Treasure Act
of 1996

commissioned by
Stephen Aylett

company
Butterworth & Co
Ltd

client
New Law Journal

agent
Ian Fleming and
Associates
72-74 Brewer Street
London
W1R 3PH
t: 0171 734 8701

satoshi kambayashi

Flat 2
40 Tisbury Road
Hove
East Sussex
BN3 3BA
t: 01273 771539
f: 01273 771539
pager: 01426 131519

title
Little Chef belongs to the Granada Group, too!

medium
India ink and watercolour

purpose of work
Editorial illustration for a food column

brief
To produce an illustration for a food column about the two extremes of the Granada Empire - Savoy River Room and the Little Chef

commissioned by
Tom Reynolds

company
The Express Newspapers plc

client
The Sunday Express Magazine

agent
Ian Fleming and Associates
t: 0171 734 8701

title
The Career Lies

medium
India ink and watercolour

purpose of work
Editorial for *Elle* German edition

brief
Illustrate career lies for women. This one is about the common belief that having a baby ruins a woman's career

commissioned by
Karin Ecker-Spaniol

company
Burda/Elle Verlag

client
Elle German Edition

agent
Ian Fleming and Associates
t: 0171 734 8701

gary kaye

Clockwork Studios
38b Southwell Road
London
SE5 9PG

t: 0171 274 1958
f: 0171 738 3743

title
Sixty Somethings

medium
Collage, gouache,
and coloured
pencils

purpose of work
Editorial

brief
To illustrate an
article on the
youthfulness and
the spending
power of the 60+
age group in
today's society

commissioned by
Alison Hughes

company
East Central
Studios

client
Viewpoint
Magazine,
Amsterdam

title
Portobello

medium
Collage, gouache,
and coloured
pencils

purpose of work
Editorial

brief
To illustrate the
feel of Portobello
Road

paul leith

37 Therapia Road
London
SE22 0SF

t: 0181 693 8886
f: 0181 693 8886

85

GB

title
Hong Kong
medium
Acrylic and paper
purpose of work
Book review cover

brief
Illustrate book
review for *The
Economist*
Magazine
commissioned by
The Economist
agent
Jacqui Figgis
Unit 4
Eel Brook Studios
125 Moore Park
Road
London
SW6 4PS
t: 0171 610 9933

georgios manoli

397
Whalebone Lane
North Chadwell
Heath, Romford
RM6 6RH

t: 0181 597 2457
f: 0181 597 2457

86

GB

title
Helping Hand
medium
Acrylic
purpose of work
Editorial

brief
Illustrate article
recognizing nurses'
contribution in
building towards
client-centred care
in high security
hospitals

commissioned by
Nursing Times
Magazine

james marsh

21 Elms Road
London
SW4 9ER

t: 0171 622 9530
f: 0171 498 6851

title
Ice Age Politics

medium
Acrylic on canvas

purpose of work
Magazine feature

brief
Ecology feature
discussing the
environment and
endangered species

commissioned by
Susan Buchanan

company
Prospect magazine

shane mc gowan

Studio 204
Cable Street Studios,
Thames House
566 Cable Street
London
E1 9HB

t: 0171 791 2916
f: 0171 791 2916

88
GB

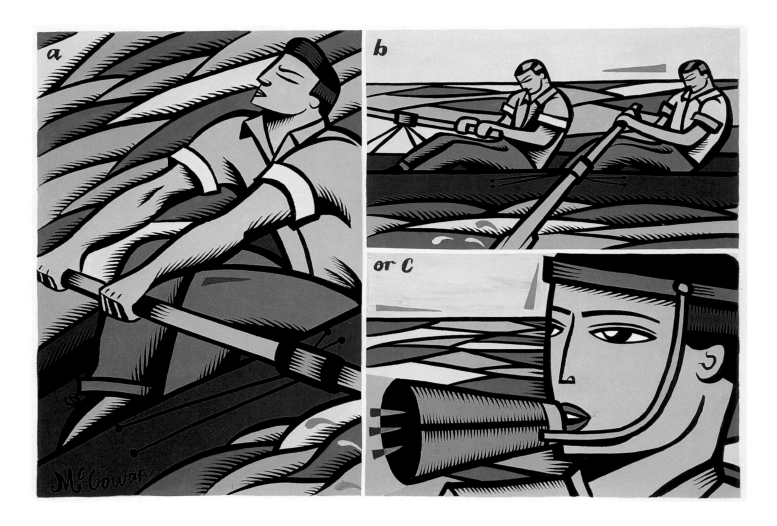

title
Tinker, Tailor, Sole Trader, Partner...
medium
Gouache
purpose of work
To illustrate article in business section

brief
To show that in setting up a business, you can be sole trader, a partner or a company
commissioned by
Andy Bevan
company
The Observer
agent
The Organisation
69 Caledonian Road
London
N1 9BT
t: 0171 833 8268

shane mc gowan

Studio 204
Cable Street Studios,
Thames House
566 Cable Street
London
E1 9HB

t: 0171 791 2916
f: 0171 791 2916

89

GB

title
Be a Rock and
Listen
medium
Gouache
purpose of work
To illustrate article
in the health
section

brief
To show how
friends' sympathy
can be burdensome
when a partner is
seriously ill
commissioned by
Kevin Bayliss
company
The Independent
agent
The Organisation
69 Caledonian
Road
London
N1 9BT
t: 0171 833 8268

general books

Alison Barclay / Art Editor / Conran Octopus

Claire Ward / Art Director / Transworld Publishers

Fiona Carpenter / Art Director / Pan Macmillan

Paul Cox / Illustrator

Nick Austin / Senior Editor of Fiction / Hodder Stoughton

geoff grandfield

30 Allen Road
London
N16 8SA

t: 0171 241 1523
f: 0171 241 1523

102
GB

title
Stamboul Train
medium
Chalk pastel
purpose of work
From a series of
eight, to illustrate
the novel

brief
Scene from Graham
Greene's *Stamboul
Train*
commissioned by
Joe Whitlock-
Blundell
company
The Folio Society

nancy anderson

8A Birdhurst Rise
South Croydon
CR2 7ED

t: 0181 681 0310

title
Exploring Japan
medium
Linocut and
Watercolour
purpose of work
Book Cover

brief
The book is
concerned with
Japan's natural
hazards, transport,
fishing and
farming, industry,
pollution and
weather

MAGNET
ARTISTS

gail armstrong

1 Vicarage Crescent
London
SW11 3LP

t: 0171 228 8882

★ **award winner:** *The Daler Rowney Award for Outstanding Paper Sculpture*

title
Clown Heads

medium
Paper sculpture

purpose
Chapter heading
illustration

brief
To show how
people put a brave
face on when
depressed

commissioned by
Luke Herriot,
Sarah Mulligan

company
DK Direct

client
Mindpower

agent
Illustration
1 Vicarage Crescent
London SW11 3LP
t: 0171 228 8882

title
Swimming Pool

medium
Paper sculpture

purpose
To illustrate text

brief
To show different
personality types in
the pool of life

commissioned by
Luke Herriot,
Sarah Mulligan

company
DK Direct

client
Mindpower

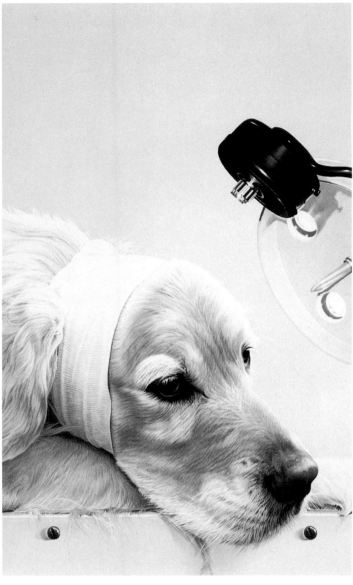

title	**brief**
Torn Ear	To illustrate a fox
medium	cub that was
Watercolour and	attacked by parents
body colour	**commissioned by**
purpose	Claire Sutton
Children's book	**client**
cover	Hodder Children's
	Books
	agent
	Illustration
	1 Vicarage Crescent
	London SW11 3LP
	t: 0171 228 8882

title	**brief**
A Matter of Life	To illustrate a
and Death	Golden Retriever in
medium	pain at a vet's
Watercolour and	table
body colour	**commissioned by**
purpose	Padd Cookson
Children's book	**client**
cover	Hodder Children's
	Books
	agent
	Illustration
	1 Vicarage Crescent
	London SW11 3LP
	t: 0171 228 8882

david bird

3 Natal Road
London
SW16 63A

t: 0181 769 5011

title
Letter back to
Ancient China

medium
CLC

purpose of work
Book cover

brief
Book cover design

commissioned by
Eric Lane

company
Dedalus

michael bramman

104 Dudley Court
Upper Berkeley St
London
W1H 7PJ

t: 0171 723 3564
f: 0171 723 3564

107

GB

title
A Regular Guy

medium
Acrylic

purpose of work
Book cover

brief
Read manuscript and produce an illustration that reflects and is sympathetic to the story

commissioned by
Kristina Langheim

company
Pentagram Design Ltd

client
Faber & Faber

title
Bright Angel Time

purpose
Book Cover

medium
Acrylic

brief
Read manuscript and produce an illustration that reflects and is sympathetic to the story

commissioned by
Kristina Langheim

company
Pentagram Design Ltd

client
Faber & Faber

paul burgess

73 Pascoe Road
London
SE13 5JE

t: 0181 852 1600
f: 0181 852 1600

☆ *images 22* exhibitor

108
GB

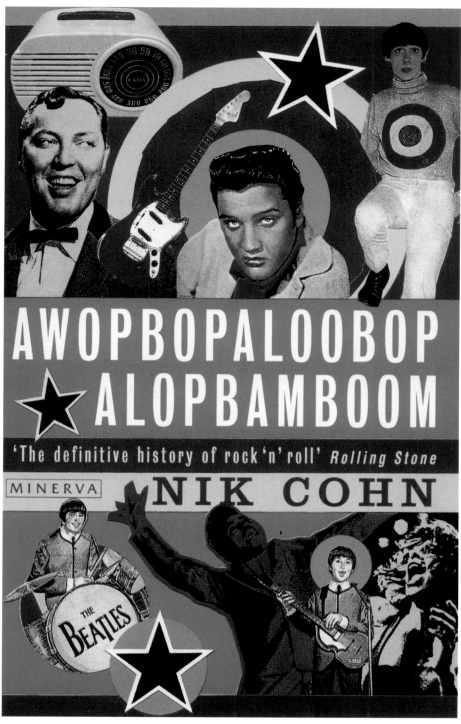

title
Awopbopaloobop
alopbamboom

medium
Collage

purpose of work
Paperback book
cover

brief
To produce a 'pop-
art'-based image
showing the range
of musical artists
featured in Nik
Cohn's writing

commissioned by
Jonathan Gray

company
Button Design/Reed
Books

agent
Private View
26 Levendale Road
London
SE23 2TW
t: 0181 291 1110

sara fanelli

Flat 11
Howitt Close
Howitt Road
London NW3 4LX

t: 0171 483 2544
f: 0171 483 2544

title
Family Terrorists by
A Nelson

medium
Collage

purpose of work
Book cover

brief
Book cover

commissioned by
Fiona Carpenter

company
Picador

geoff grandfield

30 Allen Road
London
N16 8SA

t: 0171 241 1523
f: 0171 241 1523

☆ *images 22* exhibitor

110
GB

title
The Confidential
Agent No 2

medium
Chalk pastel

purpose of work
From a series of
eight, to illustrate
the novel

brief
Scene from Graham
Greene's *The
Confidential Agent*

commissioned by
Joe Whitlock-
Blundell

company
The Folio Society

geoff grandfield

30 Allen Road
London
N16 8SA

t: 0171 241 1523
f: 0171 241 1523

title
A Gun for Sale

medium
Chalk pastel

purpose of work
From a series of eight, to illustrate the novel

brief
Scene from Graham Greene's *A Gun For Sale*

commissioned by
Joe Whitlock-Blundell

company
The Folio Society

paul powis

31 Diglis Road
Worcester
WR5 3BW

t: 01905 357 563
f: 01905 357 563

☆ *images 22* exhibitor

title
Two Trees

medium
Acrylic

purpose of work
Book illustration

brief
Painting using bold
shapes and strong
colour

commissioned by
Hazel Harrison

company
Quarto Publishing

paul powis

31 Diglis Road
Worcester
WR5 3BW

t: 01905 357 563
f: 01905 357 563

119

GB

title
Polish chess
players in
Kensington
Gardens
medium
Acrylic
purpose of work
book illustration

brief
Paint figures in a
landscape, in a
simplified way
commissioned by
Hazel Harrison
company
Quarto Publishing

daniel pudles

8 Herschell Road
London
SE23 1EG

t: 0181 699 8540
f: 0181 699 8540

120
GB

title
Vital Lies, Simple
Truths
medium
Print from woodcut
purpose of work
Cover illustration

brief
An analysis on the
ways we deceive
ourselves
company
Bloomsbury
client
William Webb

matthew richardson

Garden Cottage
Penpont
Brecon, Powys
LD3 8EU

t: 01874 636 269
f: 01874 636 269

GB

title
How Babies
Become Conscious
(The Secret
Language of the
Mind)

medium
Mixed media

purpose of work
Book chapter
illustration

brief
When babies are
born they are not
conscious of
themselves as
separate entities.
As they develop,
they learn the
boundaries between
themselves and
other people and
objects

commissioned by
Paul Reid

company
Mitchell Beazley
DBP

company
Duncan Baird
Publishers

agent
Jacqui Figgis
Unit 4
Eel Brook Studios
125 Moore Park
Road London
SW6 4PS
t: 0171 610 9933

information & technical

Tony Blurton / Director / Four IV

Janette Earney / Freelance Art Director

Jayne Jones / Project Art Director / Dorling Kindersley

Don Jessop / Architectural Illustrator

Anthony Johnson / Senior Designer / Michael Peters Ltd

title
David Beard and Friends

medium
Acrylics on canvas

brief
Paint a picture of the reception area to hang in the reception area

tilly northedge

10 Barley Mow
Passage
London
W4 4PH

t: 0181 994 6477
f: 0181 995 3049

AOI Kall Kwik

★ **information section winner**
★ **winner:** *AOI/Kall Kwik Illustrator Award*
☆ *images 22* exhibitor

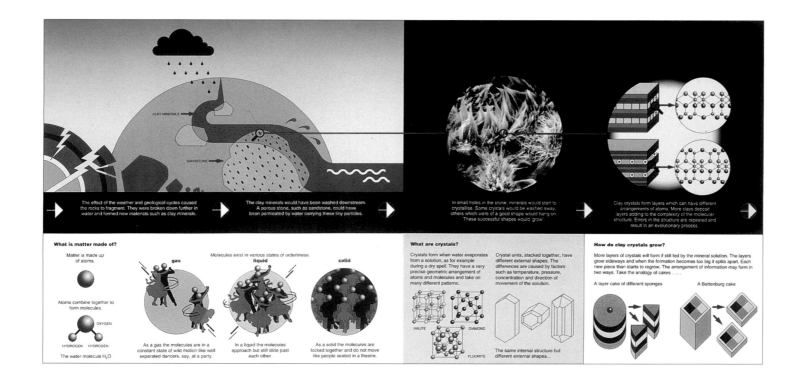

Jane Ryan / Design Manager / Royal Mail

David Pearce / Managing Director / Tatham Pearce Design

Paul Leith / Illustrator

Andrew King / Creative Director / Landor Associates

Susan Buchanan / Partner / Buchanan-Davey

satoshi kambayashi

Flat 2
40 Tisbury Road
Hove
East Sussex
BN3 3BA

t: 01273 771539
f: 01273 771539
pager: 01426 131519

140
GB

title
Summersault/July

medium
India ink and
watercolour

purpose of work
Calendar

brief
Produce an
illustration for July
in the corporate
calendar

commissioned by
Setsuko Ikeda

company
Direct Image

agent
Ian Fleming and
Associates
72-74 Brewer
Street, London
W1R 3PH
t: 0171 734 8701

lesley buckingham

c/- CIA
36 Wellington
Street
London
WC2E 7BD

t: 0171 240 8925
f: 0171 836 1177

title
A Floral
medium
Acrylic
purpose of work
In-house card

brief
Valentine's
packaging
commissioned by
Phil Cleever et al
client
Phil Cleever
agency
CIA
36 Wellington
Street
London
WC2E 7BD
t: 0171 240 8925

rowan barnes-murphy

Crossing Cottage
North Charford
Fordingbridge
Hants
SP6 2DS

t: 01725 512 774
f: 01725 512 759

title
Savoy Gala
Invitation

medium
Pen, ink,
watercolour, crayon

purpose of work
Charity 'do'

brief
Re-use suitable
characters to
amuse in a stylistic
way

commissioned by
Frances Roach

company
Buckmans

client
The Douglas
Llambias Group of
Companies

rowan barnes-murphy

Crossing Cottage
North Charford
Fordingbridge
Hants
SP6 2DS

t: 01725 512 774
f: 01725 512 759

title
All About
Performance and
Development

medium
Pen, ink,
watercolour, crayon

purpose of work
Bexley Heath
brochure

brief
"Before" and
"After" cartoons
hinting at the
benfits of a new
management
development
scheme

commissioned by
Alex Fea
TMP Worldwide

title
All About
Performance and
Development

medium
Pen, ink,
watercolour, crayon

purpose of work
Bexley Heath
brochure

brief
"Before" and
"After" cartoons
hinting at the
benfits of a new
management
development
scheme

commissioned by
Alex Fea
TMP Worldwide

sara hayward

31 Diglis Road
Worcester
WR5 3BW

t: 01905 357 563
f: 01905 357 563

150
GB

title
Pop Art
medium
Watercolour and
coloured pencil
purpose of work
Postcard
illustration

brief
To promote the
Whitbread's Pub
'Art Wimpenny's' in
Leeds
commissioned by
Mark Currie
company
Brahm Agency
client
Whitbread

sara hayward

31 Diglis Road
Worcester
WR5 3BW

t: 01905 357 563
f: 01905 357 563

title
Art Nouveau

medium
Watercolour and
coloured pencil

purpose of work
Postcard
illustration

brief
To promote the
Whitbread's Pub
'Art Wimpenny's'
in Leeds

commissioned by
Mark Currie

company
Brahm Agency

client
Whitbread

brian grimwood

36 Wellington St
London
WC2E 7BD

t: 0171 240 8925
f: 0171 836 1177

152

GB

title
The Faun

medium
Gouache

purpose of work
T-shirt design

brief
A T-shirt design

commissioned by
Cream Tea Limited

agent
CIA
36 Wellington
Street
London
WC2E 7BD
t: 0171 240 8925
email:
c.illustrationa@
dail.pipex.com

bruce ingman

c/- Heart
1 Tysoe Street
London
EC1R 4SA

t: 0171 833 4447
f: 0171 833 4446

title
Understanding the
Client Brief
medium
Gouache - collage
purpose of work
Illustrate article in
'The Atticus File'

brief
A better
understanding of
the client brief
commissioned by
David Freeman
company
Sampson Tyrrell
client
WPP Group plc
commissioned by
David Freeman

satoshi kambayashi

Flat 2
40 Tisbury Road
Hove
East Sussex
BN3 3BA

t: 01273 771539
f: 01273 771539
pager: 01426 131519

154
GB

title
Children's Event

medium
India ink and
watercolour

purpose of work
South Bank
brochure/calendar

brief
Produce an
illustration for
Children's Events
section of South
Bank Centre's
calendar

commissioned by
John Pasche,
Paul Rollo

company
Royal Festival Hall

agent
Ian Fleming and
Associates
72-74 Brewer
Street, London
W1R 3PH
t: 0171 734 8701

patrick macallister

15 Lauderdale
House
Gosling Way
London
SW9 6JS

t: 0171 582 3344
f: 0171 582 3344

155

GB

title
The Economic
Forecast Predicts
Choppy Waters
Ahead

medium
Crayon, watercolour

purpose of work
Quarterly report

brief
To convey the 'ups
and downs' of the
economic markets,
incorporating a
globe

commissioned by
Beatrice Maechler

company
Frontpage AG

client
Swiss Banking
Corporation

agent
Vetlibergstrasse 132
CH-8045 Zurich
Switzerland
t: 41 1-45753 13

clare mackie

21A Ursula Street
London
SW11 3DW

t: 0171 223 8649
f: 0171 223 8649

title
The New Arrival

medium
Watercolour and ink

purpose of work
Greetings card

brief
To create a 'New Baby' card

commissioned by
Katherine Pierce

company
Graphique de France

title
The Christmas Tree

medium
Watercolour and ink

purpose of work
Cover for Christmas catalogue

brief
To design a cover for the 1996 Neiman Marcus Christmas catalogue

commissioned by
Eddie Nunns

company
Neiman Marcus

title
The Jester

medium
Watercolour and ink

purpose of work
Greetings card

brief
To create a Valentine's card

commissioned by
Katherine Pierce

company
Graphique de France

agent
Eileen McMahon and Co
PO Box 1062
Bayonne
New Jersey
07002
USA
t: 001 201 436 4362

PRINT & DESIGN

james marsh

James Marsh
21 Elms Road
London
SW4 9ER

t: 0171 622 9530
f: 0171 498 6851

157

GB

title
Looking Forward -
Looking Back
medium
Acrylic on canvas
purpose of work
Annual report -
cover

brief
To produce an
image around the
title for a 1996
report
commissioned by
Chris Passehl
company
Passehl Design
client
Orion Insurance
Company

title
Interactivity
medium
Acrylic on canvas
purpose of work
Annual report

brief
One of six images
for 1996 report -
illustration to fit
with title and text
commissioned by
Chris Passehl
company
Passehl Design
client
Orion Insurance
Company

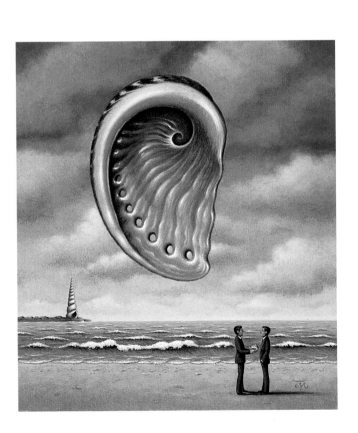

title
Communication
medium
Acrylic on canvas
purpose of work
Annual report

brief
One of six images
for 1996 report -
illustration to fit
with title and text
commissioned by
Chris Passehl
company
Passehl Design
client
Orion Insurance
Company

ed bryant

c/- Central
Illustration Agency
36 Wellington
Street
London WC2E 7BD

t: 0171 240 8925
f: 0171 836 1177

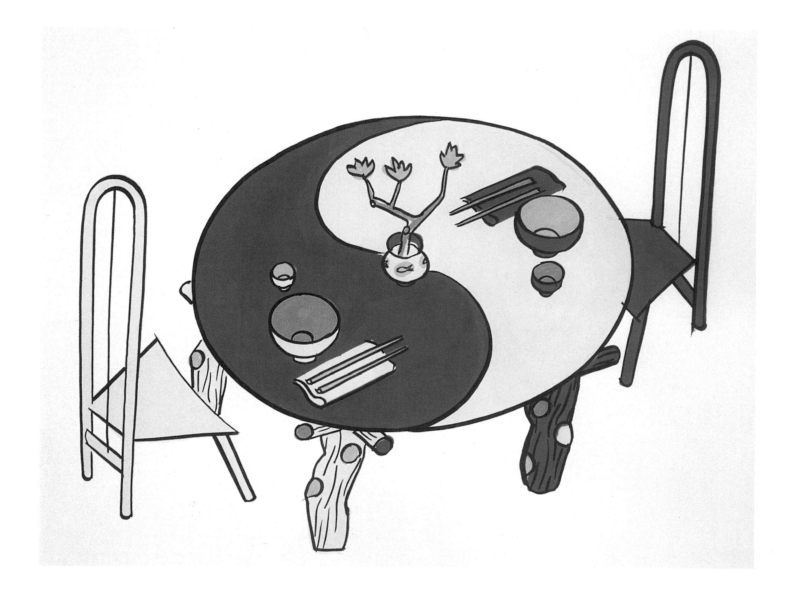

title
Yin-Yang Table
medium
Gouache
purpose of work
Illustrate article in
'The Atticus File'

brief
Observing cultural
traditions and
protocol when
working in China
commissioned by
David Freeman
Creative Director
company
Sampson Tyrrell
client
WPP Group plc

julie monks

42 Fenwick Road
East Dulwich
London
SE15 4HW

t: 0171 252 9243
f: 0171 252 9243

title
The Golden Bird

medium
Oil on paper

purpose of work
Greetings card
design

brief
Design a range of
eight greetings
cards

commissioned by
Jodi Ferris

company
Portico Designs Ltd

agent
Peters, Fraser &
Dunlop
503/4 The
Chambers
Chelsea Harbour
London SW10 0XF
t: 0171 344 1032

ian pollock

14 Crompton Road
Macclesfield
SK11 8DS

t: 01625 426 205
f: 01625 261 390

160
GB

title
Hound of the
Baskervilles

medium
Watercolour inks,
Gouache

purpose of work
Postage stamp

brief
Postage stamp
designs for the
'Tales of Terror' set
issued by The
Royal Mail

commissioned by
The Royal Mail

company
The Royal Mail
Design Division

agent
The Inkshed
98 Columbia Road
London
E2 7QB
t: 0171 613 2323

paul powis

31 Diglis Road
Worcester
WR5 3BW

t: 01905 357 563
f: 01905 357 563

GB

title
Kalimera

medium
Acrylic

purpose of work
Packaging for
Greek food

brief
To produce an arid
landscape with a
high horizon,
strong shadows
and warm colours

commissioned by
Phil Carter

company
Carter Wong

client
Cypressa

petula stone

c/o Illustration
1 Vicarage Crescent
London
SW11 3LP

t: 0171 228 8882

title
Watermelon
medium
Watercolour, pencil
and coloured
pencils
purpose of work
Greetings card

brief
To produce four
cards with a
'botanical
notebook' feel
commissioned by
Louise Tighe
company
Paperlink Ltd
agent
Illustration
1 Vicarage Crescent
London
SW11 3LP
t: 0171 228 8882

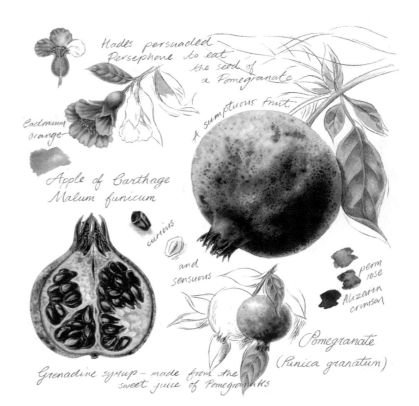

title
Pomegranite
medium
Watercolour, pencil
and coloured
pencils
purpose of work
Greetings card

brief
To produce four
cards with a
'botanical
notebook' feel
commissioned by
Louise Tighe
company
Paperlink Ltd
agent
Illustration
1 Vicarage Crescent
London
SW11 3LP
t: 0171 228 8882

michael terry

12 Bartholomew
Street
Hythe
CT21 5BS

t: 01303 269 456
f: 01303 269 456

163

GB

title
The White Lion
medium
Gouache and
coloured pencil
purpose of work
Inn sign for Bass
Taverns

brief
To humourously
illustrate the name
'The White Lion'
commissioned by
Mike Tisdale
company
Sign Specialists Ltd
client
Bass Taverns

title
Castell Mynach
medium
Gouache and
coloured pencil
purpose of work
Inn sign for Bass
Taverns

brief
To humourously
illustrate the Welsh
name which means
'Monk's Castle'
commissioned by
Richard Yarrell
company
Charby and Co Ltd
client
Bass Taverns

blaise thompson

c/- Heart
1 Tysoe Street
London
EC1R 4SA

t: 0171 833 4447
f: 0171 833 4446

title
Tribal Customs
medium
Gouache, collage
purpose of work
Illustrate article in
'The Atticus File'

brief
Depict the notion
of brands as
'badges' that cross
cultural and
geographical
barriers
commissioned by
David Freeman
company
Sampson Tyrrell
client
WPP Group plc
agent
Heart
1 Tysoe Street
London
EC1R 4SA
t: 0171 833 4447

peter warner

Peter Warner's Studio
Hillside Road
Tatsfield
Kent
TN16 2NH
England

p: 01959 577270
f: 01959 541414
mobile: 0958 531538

165
GB

title
Kitekat Leaping Cat

medium
Watercolour

purpose of work
Pet food packaging
for Europe

brief
To refine and make
more friendly the
rather vicious,
stuffed version (not
by me) of the
leaping cat I
created in 1987

commissioned by
Sylvia Vitale Rotta

company
Team Créatif

client
Mars Group Europe

unpublished

Bill Gerrish/ Senior Designer / SPY Design

Ian Pollock / Illustrator & AOI Patron

Genevieve Webster / Art Director / Children's Books, Reed Publishing

Tamlyn Hennessey / Artist's Representative / Arena

Debi Angel / Art Director / *Elle Decoration*

neil breeden

28 Vere Road
Brighton
BN1 4NR

t: 01273 700 857

172
GB

title
A Revolution is not
a Dinner Party

medium
Acrylic on wood

purpose of work
Self promotion

brief
To illustrate a
political
comparison
between
Robespierre and
Chairman Mao

john bates

27 Faraday Road
Welling
Kent
DA16 2ET

t: 0181 304 0707

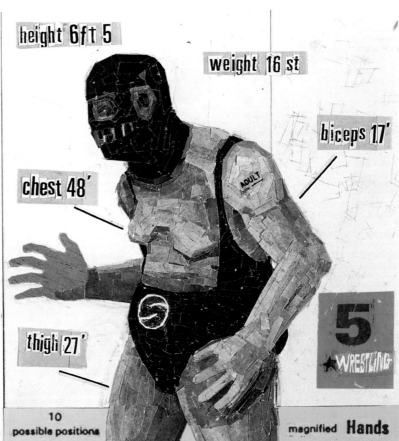

title
Wrestlemaniac

medium
Collage

purpose of work
Personal promotion

brief
You are what you eat (views on popular consumerism)

katherine baxter

c/- Folio
10 Gate Street
London
WC2A 3HP

t: 0171 242 9562

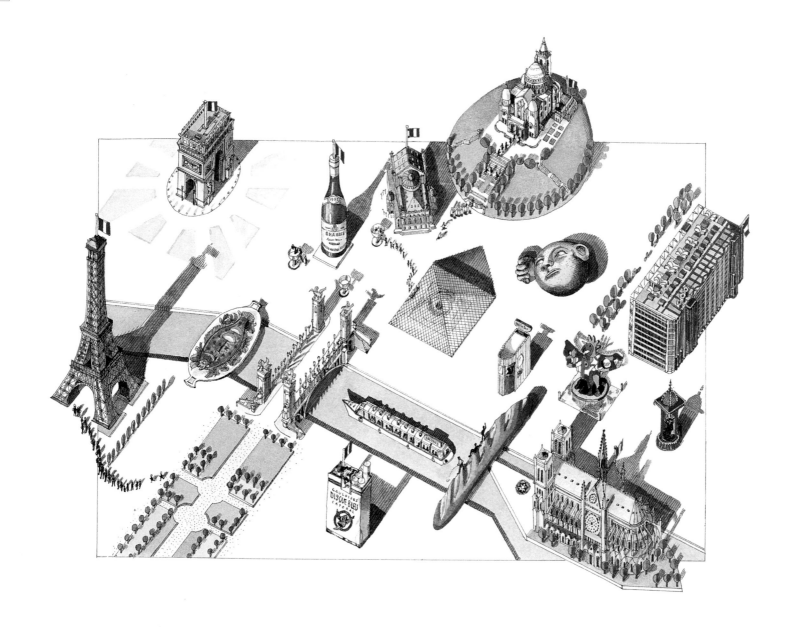

title
Paris
medium
Watercolour, pen
and ink
purpose of work
Specimen/
promotional

brief
Specimen/
promotional
agency
Folio
10 Gate Street
London
WC2A 3HP
t: 0171 242 9562

michael bramman

104 Dudley Court
Upper Berkeley St
London
W1H 7PJ

t: 0171 723 3564
f: 0171 723 3564

175

GB

title
Brooklyn
medium
Acrylic
purpose of work
Self promotion
brief
Self promotion

title
Broadway Bunny
medium
Acrylic
purpose of work
Self promotion
brief
Self promotion

emma garner

The Craft and
Design Centre
6 Leonard Lane
Bristol BS1 1EA
t: 0976 410171
f: 0117 929 7890

182

GB

title
Alphabet
medium
Mixed media
purpose of work
Personal project

brief
Speculative
giftwrap/poster
design

caroline glicksman

Geitmyrsveien 31B
N-0171 Oslo
Norway
t: 0047 911 36 656
f: 0047 22696363
(from Aug '98
contact AOI
p: 0171 831 7377
f: 0171 831 6277
for new UK details)

And finding she was left alone,
Went tiptoe to the Telephone

And summoned the Immediate Aid
Of London's Noble Fire-Brigade.

title
And finding she
was left alone....

medium
Hand-coloured
drawing

purpose of work
Self-promotional
artist's book

brief
Illustrate Hilaire
Belloc's cautionary
tale 'Matilda'

elena gomez

Stonelands
Portsmouth Road
Milford
Godalming
GU8 5DR

t: 01483 423 876
f: 01483 423 935

184

GB

title
Four Orchard Geese

medium
Acrylic

purpose of work
Self promotional

brief
Self promotional

maxine hall

1 Vicarage Crescent
London
SW11 3LP

t: 0171 228 8882 /
    01332 203 909
f: 01332 203 909

185

GB

title
Mad Cow Disease

medium
Computer

purpose of work
Exhibition

brief
Self promotional

agent
Illustration
1 Vicarage Crescent
London
SW11 3LP
t: 0171 228 8882

student